"A starkly honest and haunting memoir. Em[...]
where other authors might have drifted int[...]
tempers it all with a biting wit that at time[...]
loud. Intelligent, provocative, graphic, and heartrending, this book is
a refuge for anyone who's ever been a Lost Girl (and for anyone
who's ever been involved with one)."

> —Martha O'Connor, author of *The Bitch Posse*

"I loved *Falling into Manholes*. I adored it. How could I not? I identified totally . . . It was like being at the best meeting in the world, with
the funniest, most honest sharer."

> —Marian Keyes, author of *Anybody Out There?*
> and *The Other Side of the Story*

"Funny, frank, honest, unseemly, endearing, and challenging all at
the same time, Wendy Merrill is everything a man could want in a girlfriend, and *Falling into Manholes* is everything girlfriends want from
each other; a manifesto for the modern woman."

> —Hollis Gillespie, author of *Bleachy-Haired Honky Bitch:*
> *Tales from a Bad Neighborhood*

"Wendy Merrill is a West Coast Carrie Bradshaw whose version of
Sex and the City includes our heroine's often hilarious struggles with
commitment, bulimia, addiction, and men, men, men. *Manholes* is an
E (for estrogen) ticket ride. Let go of the rollbar and enjoy that feeling in the pit of your stomach—odds are that you recognize it!"

> —Kim Addonizio, author of *Little Beauties*
> and *My Dreams Out in the Street*

"You'll say 'Oh no, Wendy! Don't! Stop! Not again!' more times than
you care to, but the fact is, you'll find yourself caring, as Merrill slowly
gains insight after insight that eventually become powerful enough to
weave a net to cover the manholes she's spent her life falling down.
She is tenacious, observant, funny and self-deprecating—a true
inspiration." —Jennifer Lehr, author

continued . .

"Wendy Merrill has 'been there, done that,' and she knows how to write about it—with engaging wit and refreshing originality. Prepare to be charmed by this revealing, engaging, and honest new voice."

—Kathi Kamen Goldmark, author of
And My Shoes Keep Walking Back to You

"If all our lives are journeys, then this is one book you absolutely need to take along for the ride."

—Linda Ellerbee, producer, broadcaster, and bestselling author

"Wendy Merrill infuses her pages with both poignancy and hilarity—a tough balancing act to pull off! Searingly honest about her pain, yet refreshingly undaunted by it, Wendy is at once Sisyphus, rolling the boulder of addiction recovery up the mountain, and Everywoman, just looking for love like the rest of us. Rock on, Ms. Merrill!"   —Jane Ganahl, author of *Naked on the Page*

"Readers will learn and laugh.... A great, quick read enjoyable from beginning to end; highly recommended."   —*Library Journal*

"Wickedly funny and shockingly honest, *Falling into Manholes* starts as a heartbreaking journey of discovery and emerges as a beautiful, inspiring love story."

—Cameron Tuttle, author of
The Bad Girl's Guide to Getting What You Want

for kathleen.

for life.

contents

FALLING INTO MANHOLES

i had breakfast this morning with my girlfriend Hedy to celebrate my upcoming forty-something birthday. We sat in a gazebo restaurant on a beach in Maui, surrounded by palm trees and soft tropical air, and all we could talk about was aging and face-lifts. Hedy qualifies as my plastic-surgery expert, having had her eyes and boobs done in her thirties and a full face-lift in her early forties. She's fifty-three now and gearing up for her next round of surgery. After inspecting my face, she said, "If you just get your eyes done now, it might look like you've put a brand-new couch on a worn-out carpet. Wait a few more years until the whole face starts to go and have it done all at once." She continued, "You're at the age where it all still looks good, but one day, and one day soon, you are going to look in the mirror and realize that it's all gone to hell."

"Happy birthday to me!" I said, and retreated to my macadamia nut pancakes, wondering if she was right and hoping she was wrong.

It never occurred to me to consider plastic surgery until very recently. I was one of those women who took her looks for granted. I assumed I would somehow be exempt from the aging process, wouldn't care by the time I got there, or would die young. I was always secretly a bit contemptuous of women who had cosmetic surgery, thinking them vain and insecure. It has since come to my attention that whatever I have contempt for, I should just set a place for it at my table, because it's either already in my life or it's coming.

When I was a teenager I had contempt for people who drank and used drugs, girls who suffered from eating disorders, and women who lost all their money in connection with "some man." After seventeen years in recovery from alcoholism and bulimia, and having lost all my money in what I call "my spectacular co-dependent bottom of 2000" with the help of my gambling-addict ex-stockbroker-turned-mattress-salesman boyfriend, it has dawned on me that I can use my contempt, which is really my fear, to predict my future—or, better yet, to change it.

A few months ago I broke up with a younger man—let's call him Brad (since it rhymes with *cad*)—who lives in L.A. and works in the music business. He was another never-been-

married-or-had-a-successful-relationship forty-year-old man/
boy who lies about his age from Hollywood. In retrospect, this
should have been all the information I needed to stay away
from him—I wanted a mate, not just a date—but he was sexy
as hell and I had been in a penis-free zone for too long.

Thinking that this time it would be different, I used all my
powers of denial to ignore the red flags and charged ahead. I
figured if I moved fast enough, it wouldn't count as a mistake,
like if I eat a chocolate bar fast enough, it won't have any calories. My favorite definition of insanity is doing the same thing
over and over expecting different results, and this qualified.
Not unlike the main character of the movie *Groundhog Day*, I
seem destined to relive the same relationship over and over
until I'm willing to change my behavior.

My first moment of clarity came during the holiday season,
when I was giving Brad a blow job and realized that I didn't
know him well enough to know what to get him for Christmas. I
thought this was ironic, but when I told him, he said, "Yes, that
is a problem around the holidays, isn't it?" My girlfriends, on the
other hand, understood.

My next clue should have been when we were making love
and he whispered, "Women your age can't really get pregnant,
can they?"

I thought to myself, They shoot assholes, don't they? but I
was still having enough "fun" to overlook his comment.

The last time I saw him was when he casually mentioned,
"I want to marry someone *exactly* like you, only younger." This

is not something that I will ever need to hear more than once, so I said, "Good luck with that," gathered my belongings, and left.

Brad was like an abbreviated version of my love affair with drinking. At first it was fun, then it was fun with problems, and finally it was just problems. I stopped drinking years ago, but I still fall into the occasional manhole. At least I usually don't set up house and furnish it anymore. I was never a serial dater, but I was a serial mater, so after hooking up with the wrong person, I would either marry him or spend years trying to make it work. Now I can usually fall into and climb out of a manhole in about six weeks, tops. Once in a while, I can even walk around one. I call this expiration dating—relationships that last about as long as a carton of refrigerated soy milk.

My married-with-children, mental-health-professional sister Robin describes my dating history as "Wendy's catch-and-release program." I used to think this was funny, until I realized that I was guilty of the very thing that I accuse men of. The possibility of a man is more interesting to me than the man himself. If I settle on someone, then the possibility is lost. When I drank, I chose men who drank more than I did so that they could be identified as the ones in need of help and I didn't have to look at my own behavior. This "thinking" has clearly followed me into sobriety. So who's really on the hook here? What is it that I am really fishing for?

The day after walking away from Brad, my ob-gyn called to tell me that I was in perimenopause. Men-o-*pause*. The coincidence wasn't lost on me, but I was startled. How did this happen? What did this mean?

Not surprisingly, my first concern was not losing the ability to have children or getting osteoporosis but the "sudden onset and appearance of aging." My doctor assured me that, other than irregular periods, I didn't have any symptoms of menopause yet and that I was going to age along the same progression that I always have. If I look ten years younger than I am now, in ten years I'm still likely to look ten years younger than I will be. I wonder what forty-something looks like at fifty-something.

Still, I was somewhat shocked by my reaction. Is the reality of aging *that* disturbing to me, or am I freaking out about menopause and using the idea of cosmetic surgery as yet another way to avoid truly being, and seeing, me? Sometimes it feels as though I'm on a blind date with myself and I'm too shy to look up or speak. Do I really need to see my beauty reflected in the face of another to feel that I am loved?

My artist friend Tim says that the death of an idea for a painting begins with the first brushstroke. By the time the painting is finished, it has become something that may not even resemble the original idea. Having been created, it then becomes a thing on its own, with a life of interpretation independent of the creator. Perhaps my perceptions of men, menopause, and myself are like that, just reflections of the death of my old ideas that are now subject to the interpretation of my observer. The idea that I need a man in my life in order to feel beautiful, the idea of what getting older will mean, and the idea that my value as a woman is dependent upon my looks.

So maybe I'll get that eye job, and maybe I won't. But whatever I do, I'll know that beauty lives in the eye of the beholder, and the beholder that matters—I'm coming to see—is me.

falling into manholes is the story of how I finally managed to reach this hard-won conclusion and so many others in my decidedly skewed, in-recovery-from-everything, good girl/bad girl (crazy girl) way as I search for love, sex, sanity, and myself. As you will see, there are many detours. I am by no means perfect and have spent a good deal of time in a not-so-civil war with myself as I've tried to find my way. (Maybe that's why I love the line "If you find my way, will you return it?" from the book *The Phantom Tollbooth*.) You might want to brace yourselves; these are *embarrassingly* honest tales, some of which I have been reluctant to admit, even to myself, until now. If you are a man reading this, I think you are very brave. If you are a woman, I hope that you can relate to some of it, and if not, that you at least get a kick out of it, because, in the end, this *men*moir seeks to provide what we all need more of: a good laugh, an easy read, and hope.

But first, as they say, we must begin at the beginning. . . .

FIRST BORN

my parents' lives were neatly choreographed. Both spawned from German and English descent, they were the same age, grew up in the same town in Wisconsin, dated in college in Michigan, fell in love, and got married the day after college graduation, twenty-two-year-old virgins. Both were intellectuals and pursued and achieved everything they set out to accomplish. They each earned several advanced degrees on schedule, planned and executed each of their four children with precision (except for my sister Robin, who is attributed to a miscalculation in ovulation on my mother's part), and both landed in educational professions. My father, Dick, was a science and math teacher turned curriculum consultant; my mother, Kathleen, a children's librarian. They had four beautiful blond little girls within six years. As first born, I was considered the "experimental model," and in keeping with my parents' sense of order (and humor), my baby announcement read like a scientific discovery.

CASE HISTORY

NAME: Wendy Ann Merrill

DATE OF BIRTH: April 19 (3:53 a.m.)

SEX: Female

WEIGHT: 7 lbs. 4 ozs.

APPEARANCE: Resembles Winston Churchill.

INTELLIGENCE: Not yet reliably determined.

FAMILY BACKGROUND: Has heretofore led sheltered life.

SERIOUS PROBLEMS: None yet.

PROGNOSIS: Rosy.

NOTES: Appears to be a whole child having physical, psychological, social, and perhaps emotional needs. Well endowed with individual differences.

As all of you are aware, the partnership of Merrill and Merrill has, for about nine months, been engaged in forming an intricate synthesis involving carefully controlled conditions, considerable patience, and no little inconvenience and discomfort on the part of Mrs. Merrill, who provided most of the work and all of the labor involved in the project. Having threatened to do so several times during the past few weeks, the reaction proceeded smoothly and irreversibly to completion at Presbyterian Hospital, New York, New York.

The product, as predicted, belongs to the class of organic compounds known as Nascent Human Infants. The isomeric form is female, and the compound has been designated Wendy Ann Merrill. The unit mass on separation from the parent compound was 3.3 kilograms, but this is expected to increase with time as further polymerization takes place. The volume is not yet accurately determined and usually leaks while being filled. The color is a healthy deep pink, and the compound alternates between periods of extreme activity and periods of almost complete inertness. No formula has been assigned, as it has proved unnecessary.

While this is not by any means the first successful synthesis of this type on record, and future similar syntheses are planned by the partnership, the Merrills assert with pride and assurance that their product, Wendy Ann, is unique and will never be duplicated.

I'm told I was conceived in bed one morning right after my mother checked the clinical thermometer with which she had been monitoring her temperature to determine the precise time of ovulation. My father reports that he was happy to cooperate. Exactly nine months later, I was placed in the arms of my mother on the Upper West Side of Manhattan, where my father was getting his Ph.D. at Columbia University. We lived on

122nd Street between Broadway and Amsterdam by Riverside Park, and although I lived there for only a short time, it was apparently long enough to develop a New York attitude. We moved to California when I was sixteen months old, and my parents would periodically send out well-typed updates to interested parties. One in particular reported:

At just twenty-two months, Wendy is a delightful, exasperating little doll. Vicki [my sister] is an inch shorter and two pounds lighter than Wendy was at that age, and she shows signs of being a Dick-Kathleen–type child [well-behaved and scholarly]. Wendy is unmistakably a Bob-Phyllis type [my dad's sister and her husband, who were creative, flamboyant, emotional, and volatile alcoholics]. [My Aunt Phyllis eventually got sober and came out of the closet as a lesbian when she was forty-eight. I loved her!] Her favorite tricks at the moment are spitting at people, unzipping Mommy's and Daddy's most essential zippers, and painting murals on our new walls in pencil, cold cream, lipstick, and crayon.

I don't remember any discourse between my parents when I was young. Practical matters were discussed. Emotional outbursts were discouraged. Education ruled. True to their Germanic heritage, they were very exacting about everything they did. Grocery shopping was always done on Saturday morning. The menu for the week was planned in advance and posted in the kitchen. We had French toast for breakfast every

Sunday, and Campbell's navy bean soup and grilled cheese sandwiches for lunch after church. We always had snowballs (vanilla ice cream balls covered in coconut) for dessert on Christmas Eve, and everyone had the same number of jelly beans in their baskets at Easter. We ate dinner every night as a family at five-thirty p.m., and were put to bed at eight p.m. on the dot. Television was strictly monitored, and we were read to every night. When we traveled, our VW bus was packed with mathematical precision, and we all had assigned seats. We made frequent trips to educationally oriented destinations, and I have been to what seems like every museum, factory, and historically relevant battlefield between California and Maine. My little sisters and I were all taught manners early on and were very well behaved in public. Although I don't remember either of my parents as being particularly affectionate, I always believed in theory that I was loved, and I felt like I knew what to expect.

I may have started out as a wild, naked, rambunctious child, a "Bob-Phyllis-type" of little girl, but I was very quickly socialized. Everything seemed, well, just perfect. I was toilet-trained, bathed, clothed, fed, exercised, socialized, baptized, and educated before I hit preschool, and by the time I was in kindergarten I was so rigid that I could have been shellacked.

I insisted on wearing stiff little dresses with at least three slips underneath so that my skirt would billow out around me in puffy perfection. I liked to accessorize the dresses with a short matching jacket with three-quarter-length sleeves and a rounded lacy collar and top it off with a white plastic headband to hold back my blond bobby-pin curls. I *loved* my contrasting black patent-leather shoes and insisted on wearing them with three pairs of socks to keep the smooth black reflective surface from creasing. When I moved, I would keep my hands straight down at my sides, buried in the puffy stiffness of my skirt, stand up very straight, as though mounted on a Popsicle stick, and try not to bend my feet, so as not to disturb the illusion that I had created. A Stepford child-of-the-corn walking the plank into life.

It took me a very long time to walk to school.

My shiny veneer started cracking one day in kindergarten, where I was minding my own business, neatly seated at my desk, knees together, wearing one of my crisp, puffy outfits, admiring my shiny black shoes. It was nap time, and we were to put our heads down on our desks and be quiet for twenty minutes. The teacher told us that under no circumstances were we to disturb her during this time period, but as soon as my head hit the desk, I had to pee. Being the budding people-pleaser that I was, I didn't want to raise my hand and draw undue attention to myself. I didn't want to displease the teacher either. I wanted to be, at all costs, a good girl—a *very* good girl. I was always pretty good at make-believe, so I tried really, really hard to *pretend* that I didn't have to *go*.

As the minutes ticked by, I began to squirm and peek up at the teacher in the front of the room, praying that nap time would soon be over. "Just think of a waterfall," I remembered my mother telling me when she wanted me to pee before getting in the car (since inevitably five minutes after our journey would begin, one of my sisters or I would start begging to stop and go to the bathroom). So I tried to envision the opposite. Think of a desert, or the Salton Sea (we had been there recently on a family camping trip), or chocolate cake, anything, but *not* a big, loud, wet, powerful waterfall! But trying *not* to think of a waterfall meant that all I could see, hear, and feel was water falling. When I couldn't hold it any longer, I started to cry; I was leaking from both ends now, and a small puddle formed underneath my desk, splashing all over my shiny black shoes. I must have blacked out with embarrassment at this point, coming to briefly when the janitor showed up with his big mop, followed by the appearance of my mother, who came to take me home. My first walk of shame.

I decided right then and there to get better at pretending.

It started with my very first love—sugar. I *needed* it, and my mom forbade it, so I learned to be creative in order to get my hands on it. My mother was a health food nut who made our baby food from scratch and doled out sugar like it was still a rare World War II commodity. Once in a great while she would break down under my relentless pressure in the local Co-op in Berkeley on our regular Saturday morning grocery-shopping trips, but it always involved a certain amount of negotiation.

"Wendy, put that garbage back," she'd command as I tried to hide various Hostess products among the whole-wheat bread, fresh chard, and wheat germ in our shopping cart. My mom was tough, but I was determined, and over time I came to recognize that my best bet lay in the cereal department, where sugar was concealed from moms under the guise of "vitamin-fortified" and big bucks were spent to market to children just like me. Even so, the best I could usually hope for was Cheerios, because I *asked for it by name,* or Wheaties, the *Breakfast of Champions.* I could never convince her to *go cuckoo* for Coco Puffs ("Oh, *please,* Wendy!"), or to get Sugar Frosted Flakes because *they're grrreat!* ("Give your mother a break, those will rot your teeth right out of your head!") or Trix, because *Silly Rabbit, Trix are for kids!* (This made her smile, but it was still a no-go.) She just wasn't buying it.

Then one day during my regular supermarket sweep, I spotted a new cereal that I had recently seen a commercial for—Lucky Charms.

"Look, Mom, these have toasted oats, like Cheerios, and pieces of marshmallow, which are kind of *good* for you, and see, the charms are green and red, like lettuce and tomatoes, so how bad could it be?" I implored, "Pleeeease, *they're magically delicious!*" holding up the box at arm's length for her consideration.

I don't know if it was my ridiculous reasoning or the riboflavin claims on the box or whether it was just my lucky day, but she finally acquiesced. I was ecstatic—I had scored! I waited until everyone was asleep that night, snuck downstairs into the kitchen, and dumped the cereal contents into a big bowl. One by one, I picked out all the lucky charms, returned the toasted oats to the box, and crept back upstairs. With my prize I climbed back into bed, where I could relish the magically delicious sugary moons, stars, hearts, and clovers under the privacy of my covers, licking my sticky fingers as I fell into a blissful sleep.

My sisters hated me at Halloween, because they wanted to savor their candy and eat a little bit every day, making it last. I would eat all my candy in the first few days and then plunder their stashes. My mother would lock the big freezer in our garage where she kept special treats like Popsicles or the occasional box of marked-down, day-old donuts from the Winchell's down the street. This was motivation enough for me to learn how to pick the freezer door lock and feign ignorance when she would accuse me of being the culprit. Even though I became a convincing liar, I don't think I fooled her, but since she never caught me in the act, I was never punished, per se.

She would hide the Tiger's Milk bars that she would buy as incentives for us to behave. (Some reward—carob-covered protein bars!) I would find them. I pilfered pocket money from coats in the elementary school cloakroom so that I could ditch my homemade-bread-sandwich- and-carrot-stick lunch to buy cupcakes and corn dogs (in that order) from the school cafeteria.

I started taking more chances and remember being chased down the street by a shop owner, running as fast as I could, clutching my stolen Milky Way bars, both terrified and excited. At first I would hide my stolen items someplace stupid, like under the seat of my dad's car, but I would always get caught and spanked or sent to my room. I started getting more creative with my booty, concealing my stash inside my puppets and stuffed animals or behind books on my shelf so that at least if I got sent to my room I could find solace.

I thought about sugar all the time. Planning how to get it, obsessing about how much I had once I got it, worrying about what would happen when it ran out, and then planning how to get more. Pretending that I wasn't doing what I was doing in order to get what I wanted became a way of life, but I looked like a good girl, so it wasn't hard. One thing I knew for sure: I was willing to pay any price to get my fix.

On the one hand, I was always the teacher's pet, not in an obsequious, Eddie Haskell kind of way but in a sweet, aiming-to-please, Laura Ingalls kind of way. I was a straight-A student, and my report cards said things like "Wendy is a very conscientious young lady and a pleasure to work with," and "Wendy is a good contributing member of the class. She sets a good example for her peers." One of my favorite elementary school teachers, Mr. B., wrote: "It's a pleasure to teach students that are willing, capable, and cooperative. Thanks for making this a pleasant year, Wendy, keep up the good work!" (He was later arrested and convicted of child molestation, so I'm curious now what his version of "cooperative" was.)

A friend's mother said, "Why can't my daughter be more like you, Wendy?" as I helped her clean up in the kitchen after a birthday party. (I *was* well mannered and had a huge desire to please, but I suspect that my motivation in this case was to eat all the leftover birthday cake when nobody was looking.) I was a Brownie who earned all of her badges, attended advanced educational summer classes for "gifted" children, performed traffic duty patrol at school, played in the bell choir at church, always sent polite thank-you notes, and excelled in tetherball, jacks, and marbles on the playground.

I really wanted to be liked and to belong.

On the other hand, as early as eight years old, and every chance I got after that, I would dress up in all black (stretch pants and turtleneck), paint a beauty mark on my lip, and hitch-hike to nearby downtown Berkeley to shoplift candy. I was em-ulating my third-grade mentor, a television character on a show called *Honey West* played by Anne Francis. Honey was a brainy, beautiful, blond, kick-ass female private eyeful with a beauty mark on her lip, who always wore black and drove a white con-vertible Jaguar. All the guys wanted her, but she liked to fly solo, and her pet ocelot, Bruce, was the love of her life. She en-tered her apartment through a hidden door masquerading as a wall of booze behind the fully stocked bar in her business of-fice. Sometimes she would dress up in disguises when she went undercover to crack some case, and she used all kinds of elec-tronic gadgets, like an exploding compact, a garter-belt gas mask, tear-gas earrings, a lipstick microphone, and a radio transmitter posing as a martini olive, to right some wrong. I was attracted to the seedy underworld that she frequented in the pursuit of her very own brand of justice. She was a black belt in karate, and every time she kicked somebody's ass she seemed to be wearing an evening gown. She was sassy and stylish and had a witty comeback and fabulous outfit for every occasion. When asked by a handsome bad guy where she would be later, she'd say something like "By the pool, on the shady side," while sipping a martini, wearing a leopard-print bikini. She was both the coolest thing I had ever seen and hotty hot hot, and I wanted to be just like her.

The show only aired for one year because *The Avengers* came on the following season (to me, Emma did not have the same appeal), and back in those days, there was apparently room on television for only one strong woman character who dressed in black, but one season was all I needed to activate my little eight-year-old mind. (Now, I'm sure that Honey West was not a thief, but I'm also sure that her mother didn't forbid her to eat candy, and I felt certain that Honey didn't always play on the right side of the law; otherwise why would she always wear black?)

Mostly what I wanted was to be anybody other than myself. I was tall, skinny, and awkward and always felt like the one thing in the picture not like the others. I was so self-conscious and nervous most of the time that I often had trouble eating (even sweets) in front of strangers. I couldn't accept any version of myself and would do anything to appear to be other than what I was, which was usually uncomfortable. If I could pretend to be Honey West, then I didn't have to be me. I longed to be both invisible and noticed. Part of me didn't dare rock the boat, and the other part wanted to capsize it.

I remember hitching a ride back home from one of my shoplifting exhibitions in some guy's car and seeing my dad driving toward us in his green Studebaker. He was apparently looking for me, and I ducked down to avoid being spotted. I felt bad. I knew it was wrong to hitchhike and steal, but I loved the thrill of getting away with something, and the rush I got overrode my shame. I always felt guilty, but instead of acting as a deterrent, my remorse seemed to escalate my *bad* behavior.

I learned to keep secrets early on. Even from myself. I would lie in my diary, as though I could rewrite my reality. If I liked a boy named Chris, I would record that "everyone thinks that I like Chris, but I really don't. Sherry and Nancy and Sandra like him, but clearly he likes me." Or when I stole a friendship ring for my friend Karen, I wrote, "Vicki [my sister] thinks I couldn't have saved up my allowance to buy Karen's ring, but I did, and I'm just willing to spend it on others, unlike her!" I was very polite in my diary, saying, "My mom and dad are pretty perfect," or talking about my mom, I'd say, "She is really a very nice mother and I love her very much." I was always afraid that my diary would be discovered and read, and felt compelled to record my history as a good girl, our history as a perfect family, as though these pages might someday be used as evidence against us in a court of law. I felt my diary would be my passport into heaven.

My dad documented our lives with his 35 mm Argus camera. My first memory of him was of the light meter strapped to his belt, and for years I believed that if my dad hadn't taken a picture of it, it hadn't happened. This thinking helped support my growing duplicity, and as I got better at hiding my bad-girl behavior, I could point to our stacks of photo albums to support the story that everything in our lives was just, well, perfect. There were, after all, no pictures in there of me stealing, hitchhiking, or lying. No X-rays to expose me. No mug shots. Only posed family photos where everyone was smiling under the Christmas tree, or dressed up for Halloween, on a family vacation, or happily blowing out candles on a beautiful homemade birthday cake. Tangible evidence that everything was fine. We were all happy, and we had the pictures to prove it.

My mom seemed like the perfect mother, always knitting or sewing or massaging someone or baking or braiding rugs or cultivating yogurt. She never stopped doing for us. She was very organized and productive, but at the same time always seemed to be nervously looking over her shoulder, like she was in a witness protection program and was afraid of being identified. She was always rushed. She didn't appear to have many friends, all of her time revolved around her work and family, and she never liked having her picture taken. This seemed to support my witness-protection–program theory, in which, in order to stay safe, she could never get too close to anybody, shied away from the camera, always put up a good front, and made sure that everything appeared normal so as not to draw any undue attention to herself.

Still, she appeared the stronger of my parents, always in control, planning some activity or event, and my sisters and I orbited her like satellites around the sun. (My dad was also in the rotation, just a little further out in space.) She was the boss of everybody, including our collie, Dusty, who would refuse to go outside even when we tried to drag her, but when my mom walked in the room and said, "Out!" Dusty went.

My mother was good at pretending, too. She would read aloud to us every night, and her voice would dramatically change as she assumed the personalities of each separate character in the book. She would transform into a scary witch or menacing stepmother while reading the Brothers Grimm fairy tales or some other horrible German bedtime story designed to scare the bejesus out of children in order to get them to behave. (I'm still nervous around anyone with long, pointy fingernails.)

She was also a puppeteer and made dozens of storybook characters out of tube socks that talked to us. She would reenact stories from *Winnie-the-Pooh* and *Peter Rabbit,* but she also created her own characters, including Bertram the Bookworm, a gray tube sock with glasses, who taught us how to use the Dewey Decimal System to find all the books just waiting to be read on the shelves of her library. She played with us for hours, bringing characters to life, and she, too, seemed to spring to life whenever she had a talking sock on her hand.

Once I got older and lost interest in the puppets, she seemed sad, as though my maturation was a betrayal that would take me beyond the realm of her imagination. Growing up felt disloyal.

About the same time I started my shoplifting career, I began to have recurring nightmares. In one, I was on a beach watching a giant wave coming toward the shore. I knew that there was nowhere to run and that in minutes this wave would engulf everything I knew and destroy it. In another, our house was filling up with applesauce, and we were all going to drown in it. I would wake up screaming and developed an applesauce phobia. I would sit at the table when it was served and defy it. I would not eat it, and my mother would make me sit there for hours after everyone else had been excused. I would sit and sit and sit until she finally took it away and sent me to my room. It never occurred to me to tell her why I wouldn't eat it. I started walking and talking in my sleep, and my parents would find me in the morning, huddled in a closet or asleep under the kitchen table, and recount whole conversations they had with me in the middle of the night that I had no memory of. I liked the idea of not remembering anything, but I didn't like the nightmares. It was as though the anxiety that tracked me during the day finally caught up with me at night.

Reading was another great escape, second only to sugar, and I loved to lose myself in the fantasy world of books. This addiction was fully sanctioned by my mother, and I had an endless supply of the drug. I would fall asleep every night reading, with my thumb in a book and the lights on, and I would take my favorite books to bed with me instead of stuffed animals. I especially loved stories from Greek mythology starring Aphrodite, Medusa, Pandora, Orpheus, and Zeus. I devoured *The Lion, the Witch and the Wardrobe, The Lord of the Rings, Peter Pan, The Velveteen Rabbit, The Phantom Tollbooth,* and *Little House on the Prairie.* I couldn't get enough and was always sad once I finished a book and had to return to the real world. Later on, I discovered the book *The Happy Hooker* (*not* on my mother's recommended-reading list) and forever after tried to imagine how the Happy Hooker (Xaviera Hollander) could live happily ever after with Ma, Pa, and Laura in the little house on the prairie.

I was also obsessed with horses. I had a whole collection of plastic horses that I bought with my allowance (or occasionally stole, although they were much harder to steal than candy), and kept them on glass shelves that my father had built in my bedroom for that purpose. I believed that they came alive at night, and during the summer when the temperature would rise to over a hundred degrees, I would lie in bed and worry that the horses were uncomfortably hot. I imagined they were calling to me in distress, and I would get up in the middle of the night to soothe them, bathing them one by one in the bathroom sink in cool water, feeling their hot plastic bodies under my ten-year-old hands. They haunted me, and I always had the mild sense that I was failing them.

My best friend, Karen, was a few years older than me and

lived down the street. She was exotic-looking, with dark hair, skin, and eyes, and wore fringed jackets, embroidered jeans, and hippie beads. She was ultrahip. Her family was very different from mine, and I loved hanging out at her house. Her parents were demonstrative and affectionate and their house warm and messy, and I felt at home there. Her father was something like a plumber, and one day we discovered a secret stash of his *Playboy* magazines. We would sneak them out of his bathroom and hide in the basement, sitting on barstools, eating Hostess Twinkies and drinking Coca-Cola, studying the women in *Playboy* and dreaming about what it would be like to have breasts. I was shooting for a C cup at most, but Karen wanted to be a full-on, pole-dancing D cup, and at twelve years old, she was already well on her way.

We ordered a Mark Eden Breast Enhancer from an ad in the back of a *National Enquirer*–type magazine that promised to help our cups runneth over and had it sent to Karen's house. It arrived in a discreet plain brown-paper parcel and turned out to be nothing more than a stiff metal spring with flat blue plastic handles on each end. Undeterred and determined, Karen and I took turns squeezing the thing between our palms while chanting, "We must, we must, we must improve our bust!" We were bosom buddies.

My dad didn't read things like *Playboy* or *National Enquirer*. He was a science nerd with a crew cut, plastic pocket protectors, and a bow tie, and the only magazines at our house were *Scientific American* and *National Geographic*. I felt more connected to Karen's loud, messy, *National Enquirer*-reading, Twinkie-eating, Coca-Cola–drinking, station wagon–driving, bust-enhancing household than to my polite, organized, *National Geographic*-reading, bean sprout and tofu–serving, mind-improving, VW bus–driving household.

I didn't really "get" my dad. I could communicate with him on an intellectual level, but something was missing. At eight years old, I wrote a thank-you note to a summer-school teacher and, because my father was well known in the school district, politely inquired, "Do you know my dad, Mr. Merrill? I do, but not very well." My father seemed more like a legal guardian, dutiful and loyal, than a daddy who was hopelessly in love with his little girl, and I often felt that I must have been one of those babies who accidentally (or on purpose) got switched at birth and taken home by the wrong parents. I wanted my dad to sweep me up into his arms and swing me around and say things like "Who's the biggest girl?" and kiss me and hug me and shake me and tickle me. I wanted to feel the love not just in theory but in fact. He could say, "I love you." Why couldn't I *feel* it from him? Clearly he was a "nice man," and yet I felt like an item that had been left at the emotional pawnshop. Even though I could see my father standing there on the other side of the counter, he seemed to have either lost the ticket or the desire to claim me—or both. Desperately wanting to be claimed,

I tried to appear as desirable an item as possible. I felt somehow responsible that I failed to be picked up, like a television pilot not destined for prime time.

In keeping with the educationally oriented family that we were, my dad would often turn dinnertime into an opportunity to teach us something. He would conduct science experiments at the table to demonstrate some principle or other, or open discussions for other topics, generally science related. My sisters and I referred to him as Mr. Science, or King Dork, behind his back.

I thought science was boring, but one night between mouthfuls of spaghetti, he caught my attention with a glass flask partially full of clear liquid that appeared to be water.

"What do you think happens when you shake it?" he asked, setting the flask in the middle of the table.

"I don't know. What?" I said.

He picked up the flask and shook it, and we all watched as the clear liquid suddenly turned blue. Then he set it back down on the table, and we watched as the blue color slowly disappeared. When he shook it again, blue again, then clear, and so on.

"How does it do that, Dad?" I asked, curious.

"How do you think it's done?" he replied. I hated it when he did this, answering my questions with questions.

"I'm guessing there's something in there besides water?" I said, shoving my cooked carrots around on my plate, wondering if we had anything good for dessert.

"Well," he started, clearing his throat, "you mix H_2O [water], dextrose [sugar], methylene blue [a dye], and sodium hydroxide [alkali base]."

He picked up the flask and shook it as he continued.

"When you shake it, the chemical reaction caused by combining dextrose with oxygen bubbles activates the blue dye. When the bubbles settle down, the dextrose takes over and makes it turn colorless again. After a while it either uses up all the dextrose or uses up all the oxygen, and then it doesn't work anymore."

He went on to postulate about how interesting it would be to add other elements and consider what the differentials might be, but after a few minutes I stopped listening.

I had seen what I already knew: Things weren't always what they appeared to be.

MANOREXIA

i recently watched the television show *Starved*, a dark, twisted comedy about people in a support group for eating disorders. All the characters looked somewhat *normal* until they started acting out. One bulimic character, a thin, handsome cop named Dan, who claims in group to be abstinent from bulimia, while on duty sneaks into an alley after bingeing on Chinese food and hits himself in the stomach with his nightstick to make himself vomit onto a pile of trash. He is retching away when suddenly a street person emerges from under the trash. In another scene, obese compulsive overeater Adam has his jaw wired shut to control his overeating, only to sneak into the kitchen in the wee hours of the morning to splurge, stuffing pieces of cookies and squirting Cheez Whiz between the teeth of his clenched jaw, when his wife walks in and catches him. Another character, Billie, is shown frantically running on a gym treadmill, counting the calories that she's burning off with each mile, and hating another thin woman nearby, before discovering that the other woman has cancer and is thin because of chemo. I loved that a show this sick, demented, and painfully real actually aired, if only for one season. It had that "can't tear your eyes away from an accident" quality while being funny and sympathetic. I could relate.

When I was sixteen, and very soon after my mother died (no, you didn't miss anything, I just can't quite talk about it yet), I started smoking pot. Like the next day. I didn't really like the effect; it seemed to amplify all my fears, real and imagined, of which I had many. But, at the time, my desire to alter my reality was stronger than the discomfort of pot paranoia (or any rational concerns I had about hurting my body or breaking the law). Being stoned, for me, was like watching a remake of *Night of the Living Dead.* Still scary, at least it provided a slightly different version of the movie that was usually running through my head, even if the ending was the same. Plus, I loved getting the munchies. I had always been a skinny, anxious kid who was often too shy to eat in front of strangers, but when I was stoned, my anxiety took a short break, leaving my throat relaxed enough to swallow and a big, empty, anxiety-shaped void demanding to be filled. So I would smoke pot and drive to Albertson's bakery, buy a dozen cupcakes with thick buttercream (lard) frosting, and sit in the parking lot, in my '65 Oldsmobile, listening to the radio and eating them. All of them.

Around this same time, I started working out at a gym. After a few months of pot-inspired cupcake consumption, I'd finally gained a little weight. At 150 pounds and six-feet-one, I still was considered slightly underweight by normal standards. I remember the precise moment when one of the trainers at the gym pinched my budding love handles and said, "You need to get rid of this belly fat and tighten up." I was horrified. I was traumatized. Something clicked in my mind, like a gun cocking, and *bam,* just like that, I went from being the kid who always thought of herself as too skinny and never able to gain weight to the fat girl. Instant eating disorder, just add words. This was during the late seventies, and diseases like anorexia had not yet infiltrated popular consciousness, but they had just wormed their way into mine, and, like being exposed to a deadly virus, I was infected.

When nonalcoholics drink too much, they claim they feel like they are *losing* control, but when alcoholics drink too much, they feel like they are *gaining* control. That's what anorexia felt like to me—gaining control. My weight was something that I could *do* something about. I became like a guinea pig for my obsession, and like any good scientist conducting an experiment, I sought to control and document the variables. I stopped smoking pot every day and employed my constant anxiety, like an assistant, to help me monitor my behavior. I

called her Annie. Annie and I carefully measured my food and
my body each day and kept detailed records in a black note-
book with neat cursive handwriting describing my consumption and the corresponding results. I counted every calorie and
factored in potential variables, such as exercise and sleep, looking for just the right balance. Watching my weight drop felt
productive, like I was accomplishing something useful, and
while I wasn't exactly curing cancer, I relished having a handle
on losing my love handles.

Ironically, the thinner I got, the fatter I thought I looked.
When I stared at my body in the mirror, I could almost hear,
Mirror, mirror on the wall, who's the fattest of them all? Every
bone jutting out of my body looked like a bulge; every muscle
was harboring fat. It was like looking into a fun-house mirror
without the fun. I became obsessed with my mirror image
and would check myself out in every reflective surface I could
find—windows, sunglasses, silverware, and when I really
wanted to torture myself, the changing-room mirrors in the department stores— always searching for some version of myself
that I could live with. Maybe it's just my reflection, I thought,
maybe a photograph will look different. So I went to a
shopping-mall photo booth and took dozens of pictures of
myself. Standing up in the cramped space, I tried to capture
every angle, trying to reconcile what I saw on the scale with
what was revealed on the strips of film, to no avail. With a growing sense of panic, I redoubled my efforts at the gym. Instead

of eating six Cheerios for breakfast, I would eat three. I measured my food twice before eating and became obsessed with documenting each and every calorie: 3 calories in a stick of sugarless gum, 2.5 calories in a grape. Annie worked overtime to keep perfect records, trying to control the outcome.

In movie theaters, all I could hear was the rustle of bags and wrappers, and people chewing popcorn. How could they be eating all that fat? I'd wonder, slightly panicked, as though I might accidentally absorb their calories through osmosis. Defensively, I would crunch my celery sticks to drown out the popcorn-eating sounds of others, and I took satisfaction in knowing that chewing celery burned more calories than celery possessed.

Each morning upon awakening, my first question would be, *Am I fat today?* My hands would explore my waistline, and my mind would review what I had eaten the day before, in order to judge if I had been "good" or "bad." Usually the answer was "bad," regardless of what I had consumed. Annie always felt that I could have done better.

After I'd whittled myself down to 125 pounds, having lost twenty-five pounds in six weeks, there was a moment or two when I felt that I had it licked, like I was almost, almost *there.* That elusive place where everything was not just *going* to be okay but actually *was* okay and I could finally relax. Then something else took over. It was like I had been climbing up the face of a cliff and just as I went to pull myself up and over onto the ledge of safety, an earthquake hit, my footing gave way, and I didn't just slip, I plummeted. I completely lost the ability to control my eating, and I started wolfing down everything in sight. I was literally *starving*. I was shocked. How did this happen?! It was as though, once I hit a certain weight, my body was a broker who executed a stop-loss order to limit my (weight) loss on a security position. I didn't remember authorizing this order, so I couldn't believe it when I was unable to maintain my dietary position. I had failed. I was a *failed* anorexic. I couldn't stop eating and was terrified of gaining weight, so I did the next best thing I could think of: I became bulimic. I learned to liquidate my assets.

It's not like I used the term *bulimic*. I thought of it more like eating backward. Rewinding lunch. Restating my breakfast. A dietary do-over. Nobody knew what bulimia was back then. Nobody knew what anorexia was either, but being anorexic was easier to get away with, much less noticeable. I could pass for *normal* in public by perfecting the art of shoving my food around on my plate to appear to be eating or by claiming to have eaten earlier. And, besides, nobody seemed to notice that I was losing weight except the sadistic trainers at the gym, and they encouraged me.

Binging and purging, on the other hand, was not socially acceptable behavior and was much harder to hide. It was not a group sport. Picture eating a whole sheet cake, a bucket of Kentucky Fried Chicken with all the fixin's, a liter of Coke, a gallon of ice cream, then sticking your fingers down your throat *with* somebody. Maybe now it's normal for girls to get together, go on a junk-food spree, and then take turns holding each other's hair as they toss their cookies, gently wiping the spittle off of each other's faces while discussing whether it was cooler to go to Betty Ford or Hazelden treatment centers. I don't know. That actually sounds kind of nice to me, almost sweet, like a coming-of-age bonding ritual to help teens cope with the self-loathing ever rampant in our society. Maybe along with college funds, perfectionist-parents will start establishing eating-disorder rehab funds for their children at birth. Maybe opportunistic architects will specialize in designer vomitoriums for actresses or supermodels or social-lites who have adopted bulimia as an acceptable way of life. You can never be too thin or too rich, right? Instead of getting together to do lunch, ladies will gather to undo lunch. Perhaps Avon will target the busy bulimic with a retching-repair line of beauty products called Blow and Go to help counteract the negative side effects of purging (also fabulous as a blow-job repair kit for the "ho on the go"), treating broken blood vessels with Reel and Conceal cover-up, cracked lips with Toss and Gloss balm, swollen eyes with Stuff and Unpuff gel and Hurl 'n' Curl mascara, and acidic breath with Spew & Renew mouthwash. The savvy marketing executive will promote puking parties, sponsored by Hostess, encouraging women to purge and then really splurge—on product. Who knows! But back in *my* day, there was no movie of the week starring Meredith Baxter-Birney shoveling cake down her throat behind a supermarket garbage bin, blowing chunks, then returning to the store moments later with fresh lipstick, as though nothing had happened, to rejoin her critical, controlling mother, who was still shopping. Nobody knew what bulimia was when I was a teenager, or at least it felt like that. Like nobody knew but me. And all I knew was that I couldn't live without it and I couldn't tell anybody about it. It was by far the biggest and most shameful secret in my life.

It was embarrassing to shop for a binge. Buying sheet cake, gallons of Diet Pepsi (yes, *Diet*), potato chips and dip, hot dogs, buns, and mayo. Convinced that the checkout clerk *knew,* I sometimes threw a package of party hats or festive paper napkins into my shopping basket to make it look as though I was just a nice girl planning my little sister's birthday party. It gave me a good excuse to stock up on drinking straws. I shopped at dozens of different stores to avoid detection. It's not like I could exactly stock up on food. If I had the food, I had to eat the food; there was no saving it until later. Binge leftovers had to be destroyed. All evidence had to be eliminated! If binge-worthy food was in the house, it would haunt me until I ate it, wet it, or put it down the garbage disposal. Just throwing food away wasn't enough. I had watched myself eat cake out of the garbage. I wasn't very popular with my sisters when I lived at home, and later it was hard to have roommates. Eventually I would live alone.

To purge means to get rid of something undesirable, impure, or imperfect, and the food I had eaten seemed to be the obvious target of this violent act. But purging also is defined as removing opponents or people considered undesirable, and along with the food, I was trying to rid myself of any trace of me—my history, my present circumstances, my future, and all the associated *feelings* of fear, guilt, and self-loathing. It was my way of starting the day over, wiping the slate clean. I would spill my guts—to the john. I liked the sensation of emptiness that followed, as though I had cleaned house. My goal was to be half alive. Fully alive was too painful, and I couldn't quite commit to death. I was a living sacrifice tied to the altar of a porcelain god.

I remember a moment one weekend while skiing with my sisters at Lake Tahoe when I was eighteen. My time on the slopes was a blood-sugar balancing act of eating, regurgitating, and trying to ski without passing out. I recall trudging to the bathroom in my snow boots, drinking straws sticking out of my back pocket, feeling the dread that always accompanied me, like a shroud, when I was forced to puke in public. I was obsessing about whether or not I would be able to liberate my lunch without making too much noise, when I looked up and saw a young couple, cheeks flushed with excitement, having just completed their run down the slope. They seemed so alive and happy, and as they pulled off their skis, they leaned in and kissed each other, shimmering. I felt the pressure of the food starting to digest in my stomach, and Annie (my former assistant, who had become the boss) tugging at my sleeve to keep moving, but I paused. And as I stood there watching them laughing and brushing the snow off each other on that vividly beautiful winter day, I briefly allowed myself to consider what it might be like to have that kind of freedom.

I wouldn't begin to know for another thirteen years.

MEMENTO

during my brief stint as a college student, I took a class called Dating and Marriage. I got an F. I went to an agricultural school with a large male population, and supposedly women attended this college hoping to get their MRS degree. It was also a school where it was purported that "the men are men, and the sheep are nervous." I'm not sure what I was doing there. I didn't aspire to get my MRS degree, I still felt like a big fat MISS, and I was a long, long way from being a MS. I also had no desire to compete with sheep for a man's attention. Actually, I do know how I was there: by accident. I had intended to go to Cal Poly, Pomona because they had a special equestrian program and I wanted to find a way to incorporate riding horses into my college curriculum and have my dad pay for it, but somehow I must have checked the Cal Poly, San Luis Obispo (SLO) box instead, and when I ended up getting accepted to SLO, I was too embarrassed to admit my mistake. Of course, I was smoking a lot of pot and drinking at the time, and my electrolytes were probably out of whack from that little coping mechanism I had picked up along the way that involved bingeing and purging.

Oh yeah, and there was the small matter of my devastation and depression in the wake of losing my mother. After she died, I imploded, and my mind was littered with disenfranchised fragments of the girl previously known as Wendy. My heart was numb in the way that a third-degree-burn victim's skin is numb as long as she's in shock, but once the blood comes to the surface and the body starts to heal, a tide of unbearable pain comes rushing in. My full-time job had become trying to avoid that incoming tide while pretending, at all costs, to appear to be okay. This turned out to be very expensive, but more on that later.

By the time I got to college and was asked the ubiquitous college question "What's your major?" I could have truthfully answered, "Alcoholism, with a minor in bulimia" instead of "History with a minor in photography" (although maybe this was just another way of saying that I was stuck in the pictures of my past, which was also true).

The dating and marriage class was listed under women's studies and taught by Mr. Bischoff, who, it turned out, was a born-again Christian, had only ever dated his wife, and had been a virgin when he got married. This was not something that I aspired to. I viewed my virginity as something to be disposed of, like a bad habit, and wanted to learn how to go about getting rid of it. I didn't see getting married as part of the solution. Although Ph.D.s were the norm in my family, my aspirations (along with feeling no pain and appearing to be "fine") included being comfortable on any barstool in the world, being able to get naked without feeling completely humiliated, and becoming a world-class lover. I was already well on my way to accomplishing aspiration number one and realized that there was a big gap between aspirations number two and three, but I was willing to do whatever it took to make the leap. This was the late 1970s, the tail end of the "free love" era, women's liberation, and the "zipless fuck," when sex was supposed to be easy and provide instant gratification, kind of like instant Lipton's soup or Folger's Crystals. Being "intimate" with someone meant that you had a sexual relationship, yet the concept of emotional intimacy completely eluded me. I believed that I could achieve freedom simply through sexual pleasure. In my mind, sex would lead to happiness. Period.

So at eighteen, with very limited experience with men and even less recent experience with happiness, I felt like I was behind the times and needed to catch up fast. Since I had come from an educationally oriented family, I figured that taking a college course in dating would give me a leg up. You'd think that sex education would have been on the curriculum in my household, but my mother died before she got around to teaching me the advanced class, and judging from her Sex 101 lesson, I'm not too sure it would have been her best subject.

When I was twelve, she left a "birds and bees" book in my room, apparently assuming that I would study it and follow up with her if I had any questions. It was like a Dick-and-Jane book, without any dicks. It started out with a picture of a hen and a cock (this may have been a clue) on the first page, followed by an egg, then a baby chick. On the next page we moved into the mammal world with a momma and poppa dog and a litter of puppies. Then we took a trip to the barnyard and met the cow and horse families. Finally, on the last few pages, we see a married Dick and Jane standing side by side. I turned the page and, lo and behold, D&J are in bed with the covers up to their necks. Getting excited now, I turn to the next page where, ta da!, you see the proud couple with a baby, and everyone is smiling. This was not enough information for me. I already knew that little animals came out of big animals. We had lots of cats and dogs and birds and pet rats and even ducks in our backyard. At one point I had two momma cats with a total of fourteen newborn kittens living in my bedroom closet. I knew how babies came out of mommies, and that was not the part I was interested in. I wanted to know how they got in. I wanted to know about *S-E-X*.

That same year my mom gave me The Invisible Woman for Christmas, not the superhero action doll but a naked see-through plastic doll that showed all of the internal workings of the female body. How embarrassing, I thought, blushing as I opened the gift and repressed the urge to get a little bathrobe to conceal her nakedness. (I hadn't gotten anywhere near achieving aspiration number two yet.) The only naked plastic woman I had ever wanted was Barbie, and she had been forbidden in our household, ostensibly because she objectified women. I wasn't sure that the subliminal message of a woman being invisible was much better, but she was labeled an "educational toy" and had removable insides, so you could take out her brain or her heart or her ovaries and play with them. I assumed it was my mother's way of answering any anatomical questions I might have, but I was mortified. All I wanted that year for Christmas was a giant stuffed pink dog from the variety store down the street, not some see-through naked plastic woman. I eventually took The Invisible Woman apart, but when I was too impatient to put her back together properly, she ended up in the back of my closet in pieces.

Since I couldn't actually ask my parents any questions about sex without us all dying of embarrassment, I honed my eavesdropping skills at school and tried to pick up tips on the playground. I wasn't a sports fan, but the whole thing seemed to have something to do with baseball (perhaps this is where the term *sport fucking* came from?). I learned about French kissing (first base) and what it meant to be "felt up" (second base) and to "go down" on a boy (bases didn't seem to apply to boys, but if they had, I assumed this would be third base). One particularly frightening phrase, "She could suck the chrome off a trailer hitch," threw me for a loop. Being able to do this was apparently a good thing, but I wasn't sure I was built for it. I had sinus issues and allergies and a permanently stuffed-up nose, and even though I wasn't completely certain what it meant or how to accomplish it, I knew that if I had someone's trailer hitch in my mouth and I had to suck really hard, there was going to be a problem. I worried about this for years.

"She drew blood raking her nails across my back" was another troubling expression. First of all, I bit my nails to the quick, so I knew that any blood involved in a nail-to-back interaction would be my own. Second, even if I had nails, I wanted to find out what in the world would compel me to rake them so hard across a boy's back as to draw blood. I did understand one thing, though, that by the time blood was drawn you had scored, and I desperately wanted to learn how to cover my bases.

We had sex education in school, but class consisted mostly of a slide show of medical drawings of the reproductive systems. I had a few sections of this sex puzzle done, but I was still looking to fill in the blank spots. I got a few more pieces when I found a book called *The Joy of Sex* hidden in my parents' bedroom. It had pictures of real people in all kinds of different sexual positions, and although this was helpful and explained some of the mechanics of the sex act, it didn't really tell the story of how you got there. Then, as I mentioned earlier, I got my hands on another book (most definitely *not* from my parents' bedroom), called *The Happy Hooker*. I was *fascinated* by Xaviera Hollander's exploits, and this book left very little to the imagination. Xaviera went into detail about having all different kinds of sex with men, with women, and then with both men and women, and these images were emblazoned in my brain (although one incident in particular involving a German shepherd is probably something I could have lived without). After reading this book, undercover to cover, it was clear that in order to accomplish my aspiration of becoming a great lover, I needed to accumulate a lot of experience—hands-on experience. But there was a problem: I wasn't like Xaviera, who was all luscious and ripe and uninhibited and outgoing; I was the opposite. I was the really tall, shy, awkward, skinny late-bloomer girl who didn't think she was pretty and couldn't imagine being wanted by a man. I had never dared to look at my vagina and was embarrassed to undress in front of myself. I felt anxious to rid myself of this shy, inhibited girl, to grow up and bloom. I aspired to be the Happy Hooker, only without the whole taking-money-for-sex part. I really just wanted to be happy. I had my work cut out for me.

So I registered for this dating and marriage class because I wanted to learn how to date, and in my mind, *date* meant "mate." I'm not sure whether I picked up this hooker terminology from Xaviera, *date* being a euphemism for *trick*, or from the freewheeling seventies. I should probably have just gone ahead and registered for some sleazy Tantra class from the local free paper or just gone to a bar, but I was *way* too shy for that and was taught from an early age to believe that I would learn all I needed to know about life through education. I'm sure the teacher, Mr. Bischoff, tried his best to answer questions from the class, but he wouldn't get specific about mating, i.e., SEX, and that was all anybody in the class wanted to know about. It was like the whole class was from the swinging seventies, and Mr. Bischoff was from the button-down fifties. We were in color; he was in black and white. Everyone wanted to know how to get a date and details about sex—the aspiring MRSs motivated to get a husband, the guys in the class no doubt to get lucky, and me, an aspiring Xaviera, just wanting some ammunition for my mating arsenal. Poor Mr. Bischoff was being asked to be the equivalent of a modern-day Carrie Bradshaw when, in fact, he was like an animated version of my "Dick meets Jane, they get married, and somehow have a baby" picture book, so after a couple of weeks I just left the class and never went back. Perhaps I should have stayed.

I had never been on a date before I got to college, but at least I had already been kissed, although it had not been the sweet, romantic, first-love kind of experience that I might have hoped for. It was with my married, pot-smoking, alcoholic thirty-five-year-old boss, Keith.

I worked at the horse stables every weekend at a lake in the Sierra Nevada foothills where lots of cowboys, Hells Angels, and low riders from the California Central Valley came to party, water-ski, and ride horses. It was a few hours from my house in Pleasant Hill (or Pleasant Hell, as I had come to think of it), and so during the weekends I stayed in a little trailer at the stables. I wanted a reason to be away from home.

Keith drove me back to my trailer one night from the other side of the lake where I had been working that day. He was high, and I remember the smell of leather and pot and beer as he leaned across the front seat of his truck and kissed me, hard, forcing his tongue between my lips. It felt fat and invasive, and I was both excited and ashamed. I pretended it was no big deal, but this was my first kiss and the effect it had was tangible. I felt weak with something that I didn't understand, something like intense need, and melted under his arm as he drove me back to my trailer.

The next thing I remember was the weight of his body on top of me in my bed in my trailer, and I struggled to push him off. I still had my clothes on, but I was scared now and resisting. I don't have any memory of what happened next, but I'd like to think that he was sane enough to respect my wishes.

The thing is, there are big gaps in my life. Specifically when, and with whom, I lost my virginity. When my mother died, it was like I was suddenly in a witness protection program and forced to relocate to a parallel universe that was kept secret, even from me. I was represented by an alias, Wendy, here on Earth, and sometimes I knew where she was, but at other times I didn't. I was literally spaced out. My first of many long-distance relationships to come would be with myself, and I often got lost on my way home.

I had always been interested in photography, and about this time I started snapping self-portraits to document my existence for myself. I'm not saying I was Sybil or anything; I've since been in therapy for years, and nobody has ever mentioned split personalities. It's more like I experienced a huge power outage, and I resided in a perennial brownout powered by unreliable generators even before the eating disorders and alcohol and drugs kicked in to fuel me.

When I was eighteen, I had my first sexual experience with a "college boy." I don't remember his name or much about him, so let's just call him Joe. Joe lived in the country outside of SLO town, and I had agreed to come to his house for dinner. I'm assuming that I met him there and that he initiated sex, because I came out of a brownout while Joe was coming on my stomach. What makes me think that it might have been my first sexual experience was the smell, the unfamiliar scent of sex acting as smelling salts to bring the scene into focus. When he came, I came to. When he finished, he got up and casually tossed me a hand towel to clean myself up with, and my brain registered the pungent salty smell of our juices, like the ocean after a storm. I looked around his bedroom with its curtainless windows exposing themselves to the forest outside and noted the jumbled college-boy décor. As I tentatively fingered the sticky unfamiliar substance on my stomach, Joe went to pee in the bathroom, leaving the door open. It's strange how one minute you are with some guy you just met, I thought, and the next minute you have white stuff all over your stomach and he's peeing in front of you and walking around naked, like it was all nothing.

Was it nothing?

He finished in the bathroom and went to the kitchen to start preparing dinner. It was just another part of his day, I thought, in between doing the breakfast dishes and taking out the trash at night. I'm sure I hadn't told him that it was my first time (if in fact it was) and pretended that I knew what I was doing, pretended to be Xaviera. Much later I would recognize that I was a natural at this, at being able to give men exactly what they wanted sexually. I was like a beautiful reflective surface. I could be anything they needed me to be, and I knew intuitively what that was. My presence was not required, my lack of attendance rarely noted. Men could see my naked outsides, but they couldn't see my insides—and I saw neither. It took me a few years to realize that I was hidden from their view, but this time, this first-ish time, I felt naked and exposed and fragile, like the Invisible Woman at home in the back of my closet, whose insides had been removed and misplaced. I didn't want to feel that way. I very much wanted not to care.

I cleaned myself up and pulled on my clothes. Feeling a little wobbly, I grabbed a broom and started sweeping the floor to cover the blush I felt rising deep within my body. I don't remember what we had for dinner or what happened to Joe.

Not too long after that, I met my first real boyfriend, Zeke. He was a shy, tall, handsome cowboy and possibly the sweetest man I have ever known. He was very respectful and polite, a real gentle man, and he really seemed to care about me. On one of our first dates, we were walking back to the dorms after dinner, when he leaned down and picked a flower and shyly handed it to me, saying, "Here's a little something to remember our evening by."

I took the flower and looked at it. It was a California poppy, all golden and hopeful and promising and proud. Freshly picked, it was still dewy and innocent and begged to be loved and put into a little vase by my bed and admired. Being singled out from among all the other poppies in the field meant that it was special and not just another common California wildflower destined to die on the vine, unnoticed. It spoke of being pressed lovingly into a memory book after it had dried to be remembered with kind eyes from the future as it aged. It was perfectly lovely. It was created to be cherished. It deserved to be wanted.

"I don't keep mementos," I said, and as I tossed the golden poppy into the street, I felt my young heart hit the pavement, and I turned and walked away.

I would get better, much better, at not caring.

THE
PERFECT CATCH

i **was a** raging perfectionist. If I couldn't do something perfectly, well, I didn't want to do it at all. To be perfect meant being flawless. Unfortunately, I was also human and therefore inherently flawed. This caused problems. (Take this opening paragraph, for example. I've rewritten it twenty times, and I still can't get it right!) As far back as I could remember, I'd felt essentially lacking yet had an intense need to appear whole. Perfectionism, in its pathological form, is the belief that anything less than perfect is unacceptable, and I was pathologically unacceptable to myself. I believed that the quest for perfection was a desirable trait, probably something I picked up from those rigid Germans on my mother's side of the family, along with the idea that if I beat myself up enough for not being perfect, it would somehow make me a better person.

It would be years before I was able to see that perfectionism was just a well-dressed thief who, given the chance, would rob me of any possibility that I might ever have for happiness.

Every holiday season my parents, my three little sisters, and I would bundle up with our collie, Dusty, in tow, pile into our VW van, and head out on our annual family trek to chop down a Christmas tree at a nearby tree farm. Each year, obsessed with finding the perfect tree, I would lead the pack, dragging my family through the mud for hours, assessing the height, needle size, color, breadth, fullness, and shape of every single tree in order to make an informed decision, to make the right choice. I was terrified of making a mistake, as though selecting the wrong tree would have dire consequences. As if Santa would come down the chimney, take one look at our lopsided, scrawny tree, and hightail it, in disgust, back up the chimney, delivering our presents to a more deserving family, my presents to a more deserving little girl. As I led my family on this forced march through the woods in search of perfection, the pressure to succeed grew more and more intense, until I was so overwhelmed that I was unable to see the forest for the trees. Yet I would persevere, determined not to fail, until my sisters were in tears, my parents were fighting, and Dusty was snappish and hungry. Eventually my mother would put her foot down, and I would consent to a less-than-perfect tree, but not without drama and tears and only if my dad promised to wire additional branches to fill in the blank spots to make the tree appear, at least to the casual observer, perfect. A good time was had by no one, and after a few years of this behavior I was barred from participating in the annual tree-selection event.

I tried to be the perfect student, sitting in the front row and raising my hand eagerly to participate, à la Reese Witherspoon. I always did my homework, worked hard to determine what I needed to give the teacher in order to receive an A, and felt that I had failed to deliver if I was given a B. I tried to look the part and dress perfectly, but I was tall and skinny and hard to fit, and shopping for clothes was a nightmare. I would get hysterical every morning trying to find just the right thing to wear to school, going through dozens of options, each one seeming to be worse than the next, until finally I would just have to leave my house, never having found the right outfit and exhausted from the effort. I believed that if I had the right answer or could find just the right combination of clothing, then everything would be okay. It never was. Suffice it to say, I was a tense child.

By the time I got to college, my perfectionism was in full bloom. I worked part-time at the nation's busiest Taco Bell, where I wore a white minidress with a large button pinned to my chest inviting patrons to "Ask me about the Big One!" and served drunk, horny college students burritos until two o'clock in the morning. "You've done this before," the manager said, impressed as I folded my very first Burrito Supreme perfectly.

I worked part-time as a maid at a Motel 6, too, and was heralded as one of the fastest employees they had ever had. This was partly because I took pride in my work and partly because, by then, I was a full-blown bulimic (which helped me manage my constant feelings of imperfection) with lots of experience leaving bathrooms cleaner than I found them. I had spent a lot of time kneeling at a porcelain throne and, as though paying homage, had learned to make a toilet gleam.

I also had a very bright future in alcoholism (which promised to help me not give a shit about being perfect anymore), and my expertise in cleaning toilets came in handy as I learned to find the balance between drinking until I blacked out and drinking until I threw up. And learn I did. I was not one of those inconsiderate college students at a frat party who would drink themselves into a blackout, vomit all over the couch, then go pass out in the front yard. I would drink to brownout, vomit neatly in the toilet, and then scrub the basin before somehow finding my way home and passing out—the perfect party guest. The Emily Post of puking.

At the same time, I was taking a full course load at school, and here's where the trouble began. For some strange reason, I wasn't able to focus at all during my classes, let alone do my homework. I just couldn't seem to get my brain to work right. I had always been such a good student, teacher's pet, and using my mind to further my education had always been one of the most important goals in my family, the most important thing to my mother and father. But now it was as though some part of my brain was on strike, closed for repairs, or gone for the holidays, and I couldn't seem to finish anything except a drink. I had always aspired to an A+; I just didn't think it would end up being my bra size. I was so ashamed of this, my inability to rise to the occasion, not to mention my small breasts, that I masked my shame with hubris. I couldn't tell anyone how I felt or what I was thinking, and I didn't know how to ask for help. I believed that I should be able to figure it out on my own, and failure to do so meant just that—failure. I may have been an expert at expelling, but I didn't want to be expelled. The idea of failing in school was unacceptable, but I could no longer maintain my Reese Witherspoon perfect-student persona, and I seemed to be morphing into early Courtney Love. I couldn't do everything perfectly, so I stopped doing the one thing that I didn't seem to be able to manage: I left school. I figured that if I dropped out before I flunked out, then at least I wouldn't feel put out, so I packed up my perfectionism, my eating disorders, and my budding addictions and got out.

I moved to San Francisco, where I got my dream job as a part-time Xerox clerk at a big oil company. I had decided that if I aimed low enough in life, I could probably exceed most people's expectations, including my own, in my sleep. When I showed up to interview for the job, the boss, Patrick, saw me walk past his office and immediately called the HR department and told them to "hire her for whatever." Apparently, he liked my ass. (This was the late 1970s, before sexual harassment laws were invented, and, besides, this was a British-owned company.)

Turns out I made an excellent Xerox clerk. I could change ink, clear paper jams, make copies, and collate with the best of them. I could hold five sets of documents in one hand and staple them with the other in no time at all. Clearly impressed with my dexterity and speed, they quickly promoted me to a full-time receptionist position. It was harder to be a bulimic full-time receptionist than it had been to be a bulimic part-time Xerox clerk, because now I was required to remain at my desk for hours at a time, and frequent bathroom trips were frowned upon. But I was a fast study and had barely mastered the art of putting people on hold when I was promoted yet again—to Patrick's secretary.

I felt that all of these jobs were beneath me. I had, after all, been a gifted child with *so much potential,* but my self-worth was literally in the toilet, and I was too frightened and confused to know what else to do. I was too tall to be a stewardess, too shy to be a hooker, and too self-loathing to be a model—some of the other career options that I had briefly considered pursuing. Plus, most of my mental energy was spent managing the coping skills that I used to manage my feelings of inadequacy, and daily bingeing and purging along with occasional drinking bouts was turning out to be a full-time job. The result was that I was the twenty-year-old secretary with the really bad attitude who thought very little of herself but was all she thought about. An egomaniac with an inferiority complex. An easy mark. A sitting duck.

I spent the next six months fending off my boss. Although I portrayed myself as someone who had seen and done it all, and would do things like sit in his office, cross my long legs, and say, "I wonder what it would be like to be a hooker," I still was incredibly naïve, fragile, and insecure. I desperately wanted male attention but had no idea what to do with it when I got it. I didn't want to sleep with my boss, but he just couldn't seem to take no for an answer. When I couldn't take the pressure anymore, I did the only thing I could think of doing: I quit my job to find something better.

The thing is, I wasn't any better, so I ended up resorting to what I knew how to do and do well: I hid out in my cockroach-infested, shag-carpeted studio apartment for months, locked in a cycle of bingeing and purging and drinking. I was miserable. I was depressed. It was like I was in training to be a professional bulimic or working on my doctorate in drinking and had been put on the fast track. My big outing each evening was shopping at Cala Foods, open twenty-four hours a day. I usually went around two a.m. I felt less likely to be judged by the checkout clerks when buying binge supplies like potato chips, cake, ice cream, cookies, and wine in a box if I was in line with a Polk Street drunk or transvestite or hooker or junkie buying liquor or lubrication or condoms or Visine. I fit right in.

I wouldn't answer my phone and didn't talk to anyone for months. I lived in a surreal state of perfectionist paralysis, too terrified to move forward and unable to go back, like I was stuck in some kind of cosmic turnstile. Eventually a couple of my sisters stood outside my apartment and threw rocks at my window until I was forced to respond and was dragged, reluctantly, back into the world.

That's when I met Bobby. At twenty-eight years old, he seemed to have it all together: a successful career in the construction business, a cute little cottage in Sausalito, and a silver Honda Accord. He was Greg Kinnear cute and pursued me with a vengeance. If he really wanted me, I reckoned, then I must be okay after all! I'd never had this much attention from a man in whom I was actually interested, never had been wined and dined before, and suddenly found that I didn't have to binge and purge all the time. It must be love!

Bobby was boyish, sexy, and fun and, as luck would have it, also liked to drink . . . quite a lot. I proceeded to get a crash course in the art of wining, dining, and making love. There was just one little catch: I was a quick study and almost immediately got pregnant. I was shocked. For some reason, I was completely convinced that I couldn't have babies. I had a whole story that lived in my head about how my fallopian tubes were blocked, the result of a hernia operation that I'd had as a child. It was true that I'd had a hernia operation, but my perception of reality was so distorted that the rest of the story could have been lifted from some made-for-TV movie I had seen while stoned and come to believe was the truth for me, I'm not sure. The only thing I knew for sure was that I was pregnant. It never occurred to me to have that baby. I was completely unacceptable to myself as a mother. I didn't tell Bobby until right before I had the abortion; I didn't want to ruin our perfect relationship. I thought that it was my fault, my problem, and that I needed to take care of it by myself. Bobby confirmed this when his response to my news was "Why does this always happen to me?" Shortly afterward, we moved in together.

The second catch was that Bobby was still pining away for his ex-girlfriend, Brenda, who had left him for another woman. By pining, I mean still writing poetry for her, still checking the mailbox every day for some correspondence, monitoring the message machine for her voice (this was before e-mail and cell phones), and lamenting her loss at every opportunity. I hated it. I wanted to be the only one, not the other woman who was coming in second to a lesbian ex. The harder I tried to be desirable and worthy of Bobby's praise and devotion, the further away I seemed to be from my goal. What had happened? Had he pursued me just to distance himself from his own pain? Did he love me, as he said, or was I being used as pain medication? Was I the whiskey in his bottom drawer? Was he mine? These questions went unasked and unanswered.

Fortunately, I had another, much more reliable lover to turn to—alcohol. Wine didn't pine for another, Absolut gave me its full attention, and Jim Beam and Johnnie Walker never let me down. José Cuervo would occasionally go south on me, but I was very forgiving and always welcomed him back with open arms. My affair with alcohol was polyamorous, and I didn't discriminate. Each type of libation offered me relief, and whenever I was with these lovers, whenever I was drunk, the constant anxiety and fear that I lived with the rest of the time vanished. I felt like everything wasn't just going to be okay, it *was* okay, and I was perfectly safe. I couldn't imagine my life without them. Even my bulimia took a backseat to the drink-ing, and dealing with the occasional hangover or blackout seemed like a small price to pay not to have to throw up ten times a day. These were my choices.

Accordingly, I switched my allegiance from Bobby to booze, and my days became more and more alcohol-centric. At work (I had returned to the oil company and gotten another job in a different department), I would watch the clock until four-thirty in the afternoon rolled around, in anticipation of a "happy" hour on the ferry ride home, wine with dinner, and after-dinner brandies into the evening. I did whatever I needed to do to ap-pear to be a functioning member of society so that nobody would throw rocks at my window again, but at twenty-one, my idea of a perfect day was to stay home from work, curl up with a bottle, and watch television until I passed out cold. It never once occurred to me that I had a drinking problem or that I might be an alcoholic. Alcohol was the solution, not the problem.

Bobby, on the other hand, started to be a problem. Like when he accused me of paying more attention to Johnnie Walker than to him. I thought this was ironic. I was compet-ing with a lesbian ghost for his attention, and he was jealous of a spirit. He drank more than I did, yet he would mark my bot-tles in an attempt to monitor and control my drinking. I thought nothing of filling my own bottles back up with water to throw him off. I learned to appear less drunk than I usually was and discovered how cocaine could help me accomplish this trick.

I went to great lengths to hide my behavior and appear to be drinking "normally," until one day Bobby walked in on me in the bathroom—where I had been pretending to take a shower— while I was doing lines of coke on the back of the toilet seat. Even I knew that this wasn't normal. I was humiliated and he was upset, but that didn't stop me. I was being torn between two lovers, and soon one of them was going to have to go.

In the end, I was the one to go. After eighteen months with Bobby, I packed my bags and moved back to the city. I started hanging out with a man I had met at work, Franco, who was fifteen years my senior, liked cocaine, and was unhappily married with two children.

If the paradox of perfection is true, that the greatest perfection is imperfection, then I was well on my way to finally being perfect.

KISS 'N' HELL

i woke up out of a blackout on the phone in my bedroom. Crap, I thought, Sabrina has been here again. Sabrina was what I had dubbed my drinking personality, named after Samantha's evil cousin on the television show *Bewitched*. Samantha was the good witch, Sabrina was the bad witch, and both characters were played by the perky blond actress Elizabeth Montgomery. Periodically, Sabrina would pop into Samantha's life, magically assume her identity, get her into all kinds of hot water, and then split the scene, leaving a confused Samantha to suffer the repercussions of Sabrina's actions. This was very much what my life had become.

My Sabrina wasn't all bad. She was the one who, determined to have an orgasm, took me to Good Vibrations in San

Francisco and bought a vibrator to educate us before we had any hands-on experience in this department with men. The fact that she practiced using the battery-operated vibrator so frequently that we would get weak in the knees whenever we heard something vibrating may explain why we often were attracted to men who carried beepers. Unfortunately, at that time (in the pre–vibrating cell phone days) men sporting beepers usually were either drug dealers or married men whose wives were expecting babies at any moment. I think Sabrina meant well; she was just misguided, and whenever she was in the driver's seat, we always ended up in a bad neighborhood.

I listened to the voice on the phone and realized that I had been talking to Caleb. I (Sabrina) had met Caleb in a recent blackout while staying with my friend Kathy in the mountains outside of Carmel Valley. He had been bartending at a little bar where I insisted that Kathy and I stop on the way back from a grocery-store run. Caleb was a sexy Cajun singer/songwriter/guitar player/bartender and sometime drug dealer. I was so drunk the first time we had sex, I didn't even notice that he had a colostomy bag, and when I woke up to it the next day, I didn't say anything, didn't want to hurt his feelings.

What is happening to me? I thought, hanging up the phone and lowering my face into my hands, which reeked of whiskey. Caleb was on his way over.

My twenties had been a blur. I had lived with two men: Bobby for eighteen months and Franco for five years. I had loved both of them but was truly in love with Franco, who had nicknamed me Beak, because he liked my nose. I would call him Beak back for no apparent reason, and we would lie nose to nose in bed, whispering "Hi, Beak," "Hi, Beak," back and forth to each other until we fell asleep. I knew that he loved me, and being with him was the closest that I'd ever felt to being safe with a man, but there had been a little problem: I had another lover, and a very possessive one at that. Johnnie Walker didn't like competing with my boyfriend or my job for attention, and when he called to me in the night, a late-night boozy call, I would answer, leaving Franco sleeping soundly, while I snuck off to the bathroom to drink the whiskey that I had hidden in my purse. Nighttime usually meant nightmare time for me, and drinking always spelled relief from the riot going on in my head. During the day, or in the presence of others, I had to control my drinking, but when Johnnie W. and I were alone in the bathroom late at night, I could embrace him the way I wanted to: without restraint, without ice, without a glass, just straight out of the bottle, until we were both gone. I loved him, and he loved me back. With this lover, I always swallowed.

I usually felt safe while in a bathroom—restroom, john, comfort room, water closet, lavatory, commode, loo, powder room, toilette, *baño, Badezimmer*—my existential exit in any language, and I'd spent a lot of time staring at smooth ceramic tile over the years. Between using cocaine, bingeing and purging, and drinking, I learned to scope out the bathroom situation everywhere I went, the same way a cop might automatically scan a crowd for suspicious characters. Single lockable bathrooms provided the most privacy, but there could be more pressure to finish if someone was waiting, jiggling the door impatiently. Chopping cocaine or throwing up took time. Multiple stalls meant less pressure to finish but more pressure to be quiet, which was fine for drinking but not great for vomiting or chopping. I lived in constant fear of being overheard or discovered. Deciding where I would go to eat or which gas station I would frequent was based on my varying toilet criteria. Vacations were planned around it. Bed-and-breakfasts were never an option.

I began experiencing anxiety attacks, and sometimes when I was on public transportation, I would have to get off the BART train and rush to the john, where I would sit hyperventilating into the brown paper bag that I had taken to carrying in my purse. At the time, I didn't know these episodes were anxiety attacks, and went to the emergency room several times for help because I was afraid that I was going to die—that I was having a heart attack—but they just pumped me full of fluids and sent me home. Nobody ever mentioned alcohol. I didn't look like I should be doing what I was doing. I looked like a good girl who was just brown-bagging it.

My father, Dick, brown-bagged it, too, but his bag contained things like turkey sandwiches and carrot sticks. Every few months he would dutifully call each of his four daughters, to check in and let us know which distant relative had died, which cruise he and my stepmother, Shannon, were planning, or what their cat, Peepers, was doing. He rarely asked about the specifics of my life, and he didn't know about the bulimia or the drinking or the drugs. Maybe he just didn't want to know. I know I didn't.

He did, however, sometimes seem baffled by my bizarre behavior (he didn't know it, but pretty much every time I had seen him since I left home at eighteen, I had been drunk or high), and he would say things like "Why can't you just be normal?" This made no sense to me at all. Normal was a setting on a dryer, right? I didn't know from normal. Maybe my dad was normal: He had a very clear sense of right and wrong, was a Democrat, a straight arrow, a go-Navy, save-the-earth, cash-register-honest, magna-cum-laude, just-say-no, don't-worry-be-happy, obey-the-letter-of-the-law kind of guy. He rarely drank, wouldn't dream of smoking or doing drugs, and always ate a sensible breakfast. He would no more have considered drinking or eating to excess than he would have considered voting for Ronald Reagan or littering.

I, on the other hand, alternated between bingeing on Safeway sheet cake and vomiting until I had pink buttercream frosting coming out of my nose, and drinking whiskey out of a brown paper bag from my purse in bathrooms just to get through the day. "I just don't have the same emotional needs that you do," Dick had said. No kidding, I'd thought.

But then nobody really knew what was going on with me. I was very good at pretending that everything was fine, and I would no more have considered telling the truth about my life than I would have considered voting for Ronald Reagan.

(At least my father and I had that in common.) I was too frightened and ashamed to look directly at my behavior, or what
might be causing it, and held everyone in my life, including
myself, at emotional bay. My three sisters all lived in different
cities by this time, and I only saw them a few times a year. My
drinking during our visits passed as part of holiday festivities,
and I was nothing if not festive. Nobody else in my family drank
like I did. My friends, however, all drank like I did or more, so
they weren't about to question my behavior, and no one knew
about the bulimia. The more I drank and purged, the more I
needed to drink and purge in order not to feel the emotional
repercussions of drinking and purging, and so on, and so on,
and so on.

After five years together, Franco and I finally bought a
house. I was drunk during the entire process. I remember riding in his Fiero after signing the papers, fantasizing about
throwing myself out of the speeding car onto the pavement.
The next day he asked me to marry him, and I couldn't even
answer. I knew I couldn't be a wife, couldn't possibly be a
mother, and that I would ultimately disappoint him. My answer
was to pack up my stuff and leave, like an animal going off into
the woods to die alone.

Only I wasn't alone for long. I didn't think I had a drinking
problem, just problems when I drank, and decided that my real
trouble was that I had always been monogamous, and that the
solution was to become polyamorous. (Although it wasn't called
being polyamorous back then, just slutty.) I was an aspiring

slut. I thought the ability to sleep with more than one guy during the same period of time (if not the exact same time) somehow would make me a better woman or a better lover or, at the very least, make me feel better, so I gave it my best shot.

I started by dating my gay assistant at work, sexy Stephen. I had been promoted through the ranks in the corporate world, in spite of myself. I had even been drunk when I interviewed for my last job, which I wasn't qualified for, as a systems analyst. (As I've said, I was gifted in giving people exactly what they were looking for and had an innately high credibility rating.) I got the job and, eventually, Stephen, when Sabrina seduced him one evening after a long weekend of drinking and dancing in the gay parade.

Then I met macho Mark, the publicist for a famous rock star, over a hot dog and a beer in an airport bar, and occasionally joined him on tour. Then tattooed Tommy, ten years younger and in the army, whom I met while vacationing with friends at the Jersey shore. Then dirty Harry, a friend of my sister in Washington state, and now Cajun Caleb. I was never sober when I met these men, always drunk when I had sex. Once they all came to town the same week, and I couldn't keep track of whom I was with or, more specifically, Sabrina was with. I blacked out often and never encouraged anyone to tell me what had happened. I just pretended everything was fine. Everything was not fine.

The more men I dated, the more out of control and confusing my life became, and the more I drank. I was always hiding something from somebody, and men's balls weren't the only things I was juggling. There was also alcohol, cocaine, exercising, working, drinking, bingeing and purging, and trying to appear "normal." I never slept; I only passed out. It was exhausting. I stopped drinking for a week in an attempt to pull myself together and had a moment of clarity about the way I was living. I realized that I either needed to change my behavior or start drinking again. I started drinking again. Wasn't this what I was supposed to do?

Sometimes I would take pictures of myself, drunk, and absently wonder, Who was this girl? What was happening to her? Was she having fun yet? When were we going to be able to go home?

I lived in a terminal state of vagueness, a kind of perennial purgatory. I woke up on my couch one day and saw that it was six o'clock Monday morning. Still half in the bag, I jumped up, took a shower, and got dressed for work. I was heading out the door when I realized that it had been six p.m., not six a.m., and it was still Sunday night, not Monday morning. Rather than this being a cause for concern, I was just happy to be able to go into the kitchen and pour another drink. I started to pray each night that I would die in my sleep, not yet realizing that I was already dead.

I started drinking in the morning before work because my hands shook so violently that I thought they would fly off the end of my arms. I became one of those people loitering outside the corner liquor store, waiting for it to open at seven a.m. along with a few Mickey Rourke look-alikes from the movie *Barfly*—you know, the kind of guys who looked like they had to use a pulley system involving a necktie and their hand just to get the shotglass from the bar to their mouth without spilling the contents. I had contempt for these men, but I was one of them; I just didn't know it ... yet. Wearing my business suit and high heels, with my blond hair swept up in a conservative bun, I looked like a *National Enquirer* cover: "Princess Di Visits Skid Row." Only I wasn't visiting; I lived here.

Once inside, I would ask for a pint of vodka (whiskey was too risky in the morning), trying unsuccessfully to appear casual, as though I was ordering a cup of coffee to go. I might throw in a random package of Tampax and some Pamprin to try and disguise the nature of my purchase, but these clerks were hard-core and could not be fooled. Good girls didn't drink vodka in the morning, even if they were on their periods, and there was no way to dress this up. I didn't mind my shaking as much as I minded anyone *seeing* me shaking, and was always grateful for the green Astroturf on the counter where I would place my money and retrieve my change so that I didn't have to experience any hand-to-trembling-hand exchange of money.

After a while, even the morning drinks wouldn't stop the shaking, and I had to be careful about what I ordered for lunch when I dined with others: Soup was out of the question, and anything involving a knife or a fork could be dangerous. Sandwiches were better, because I could grip them, but eventually I just started going home for lunch and drinking.

As I returned to work one day after a liquid lunch, there was a big earthquake. I didn't even notice. My body had become one big tremor, and the ground was always moving beneath me. I constantly focused on walking a straight line, as though I were aboard a big ship—specifically, the *Titanic*—being tossed around at sea.

Finally, I just ceased to function. I was sure I was about to get fired. I had stopped talking to everybody, except for Caleb, so I had him call my office and quit my job for me. I was too embarrassed to face them. It was as though my life had been performed onstage and, unbeknownst to me, the movie was a wrap, and the wrecking crew had been brought in to strike the set. All the exterior cues that I had used to define myself—my job, my boyfriends, my ability to get dressed in the morning, any pretense of sanity—were gone and I was left wearing my white bathrobe, wringing my hands, and wandering around my apartment in a state of suspended animation, waiting for my new script.

Except for my liquor-store runs, I had been alone in my apartment for a week, and although I was drinking, I couldn't get drunk. Like a vindictive lover, alcohol had betrayed me, had quit on me, and I just could not believe it! How could this happen to *me*! I shook so much that I could barely stand erect in the shower and paced my apartment like a caged feral cat, repeating, "I just want to get my mind back. I just want to get my mind back." It was very *Days of Wine and Roses,* only without the roses . . . or the wine. More like *Whiskey River,* really.

I didn't want my feelings, and they knew it. They were like needy Baby Hueys who had been ignored for years and were now deliberating, like a sequestered hung jury, over my fate. Apparently, I was the deciding vote. Was she to live or was she to die?

I started hearing phantom phones ringing, and then tiny whispering, as though little people from *Land of the Giants* were under my couch plotting their next move. I sat on the couch, feet up, waiting for them to make a run for it, and was disappointed when they never appeared. I was remotely aware that I was having auditory hallucinations, but, again, it seemed abstract, as though happening to someone else, like something I was watching on the late-night Sci-Fi channel.

After a while, I heard a different voice, the one in the back of my head that was getting louder and louder. Normally I try to tune out this particular voice, but I had been beaten down and couldn't find the volume knob. The voice kept repeating, "YOU'RE AN ALCOHOLIC, YOU'RE AN ALCOHOLIC," over and over. This was not language that I would have used. I did not think that I was an alcoholic; I just thought that I was *acting* like one, portraying one in my very own reality television series, starring Sabrina. Real drunks were old men in trenchcoats on Sixth Street, not nice girls who grew up in the suburbs. Not Samantha from *Bewitched.*

But the voice continued, and I felt like I had been painted into a corner and had nowhere to go. I was in check, and didn't want to be mated. For once, I was completely out of ideas. I didn't know what to do. Drinking had stopped working, but I couldn't stop drinking. I didn't want to live, but I couldn't quite die. I felt like that late-night television commercial I had seen for some posh rehab center featuring the little man trapped under a shotglass, unable to escape, face contorted into Edvard Munch's painting *The Scream.* My brain froze up, like an engine devoid of oil, and in that moment, I did the one thing I had never been able to do. I did the most radical thing I have ever done in my life. My absolute last resort. I asked for help.

At my boss's request, I recently had started seeing a therapist, and I called him. "I need to be medically supervised," I said. "I can't be in the world and not drink." He called me back twenty minutes later, having enrolled me in a twenty-eight-day alcohol and drug–rehab program at a hospital in nearby Redwood City. My mind briefly registered that this was not my rehab of choice, this was not the Betty Ford–fabulous spa-like environment that I had imagined. Redwood City was the armpit of the Bay Area, and I didn't want to be *hospitalized,* did I? How embarrassing! Straitjackets, Nurse Ratched, and shock treatments sprang to mind, but I didn't argue; I couldn't argue; the jury had decided, the vote was in: I had been sentenced to life.

I looked in the mirror now and hardly recognized the

woman I had become. Broken blood vessels were scattered across my cheeks, and my face looked like my liver was starting to feel, bloated and doughy—a day-old corpse. I was barely able to meet my Soylent Green eyes, and when I finally did, saw *Flowers in the Attic* children, abysmally betrayed. I went to the kitchen to see what I had left to drink. A half-pint of peppermint schnapps and three tall Budweiser beers. I put them in my purse. My version of packing for rehab. *How very country-western.* Caleb arrived, and I put on my long purple eighties leather coat with the big padded shoulders, something Prince might wear (his backup singers were, after all, Lisa and *Wendy*). We went downstairs to his car.

Redwood City was about forty-five minutes away, and I drank my way down the coast. As we got closer, I began to reconsider. Perhaps I was overreacting, I thought as I swigged the last of the schnapps. I could stay in the car with Caleb, let him drive me all the way down to Monterey, spend the weekend doing drugs and drinking and fucking—my version of letting him take care of me, make me well. But there was that voice again, the one from the back of my head that was apparently in the driver's seat now.

"This is my exit," I heard myself say, and as we pulled off the highway, I was vaguely aware that I was about to play the role of a lifetime.

SERIAL MATER

last night I watched a Discovery Channel special on the ten most extreme animals. The male anglerfish was number one, beating out the duck-billed platypus for the weirdest animal on earth. The male anglerfish is forty times smaller than the female. For many years, biologists didn't think the fish were the same species; they seemed so dissimilar. The female has an antenna sticking out of the top of her head that glows with organic phosphorescence to attract prey, and her sharp, jagged teeth jut from a mouth stuck in a permanent scream—the ultimate female shrew. The male is unremarkable in appearance but not in behavior. When it's time for the male and female to mate, the male dives kamikaze-like into the side of a female, where he stays, slowly being absorbed by the female, until he is nothing but a sperm-bank lump protruding from her side.

Now, that's what I call mating for life.

The idea of commitment in romantic relationships often feels like that to me. I'm afraid that if I ever truly commit myself to a man, I will become buried permanently in his side, slowly being absorbed, until there is nothing left of value except my eggs, and now even those are starting to expire, like the eggs you buy at the corner liquor store. Or, conversely, that my mate will be permanently buried in my side, drawing on my life force to exist and depending completely upon me for his identity.

In order to avoid either of these scenarios, I often have selected very anti-anglerfish men, who, for one reason or another, are unable or unwilling to commit to a long-term, serious romantic relationship. For a while, I blamed these men for their apparent inability to commit to a future, until it occurred to me that all my relationships have one thing in common: *me*. I pair up with these male versions of myself so that I don't have to acknowledge my own fear of making a serious commitment. *Ugh*.

Clearly, I'm not a paragon of emotional health, but it got me thinking: What does it take for Mr. Anglerfish to make that leap? Obviously, he's driven by some biological imperative, some instinct to proliferate the species that overrides his individual survival need. What are the driving forces behind *my* mating behavior? I've been asking myself for years, Why is it that I can't have sex with someone without becoming attached or falling in love, but I can never commit for the long haul? Is my instinct to mate stronger than my desire to remain an individual, or is my desire to remain an individual what eventually overrides my instinct to mate? I seem to have this little problem with commitment, yet I've been a serial mater, always half-assed involved with somebody for a long period of time or fully involved for a short period of time. Am I afraid of love? Of being rejected? Am I missing some important commitment gene? Why can't I mate in captivity?

Recently, I was at a wedding reception on a beautiful beach in Maui. My friend's six-year-old daughter, Rose, and I collected heart-shaped coral and rocks to place on every table to help celebrate and commemorate love and all that marriage represents. I watched as a little six-year-old boy picked up one of the heart-shaped rocks that we had lovingly arranged on the buffet table. Turning it upside down, he pointed to the center of the inverted V shape that to him looked like a crotch, and proudly stated, "This is where my pee-pee goes." Are men and women simply biologically at odds with each other as a species when it comes to love and sex?

Deciding to examine these issues from a scientific perspective, I did a little research. The trouble seems to start with sex pheromones, chemicals that when emitted trigger a "reproductive behavioral response" from a member of the same species. Also, many other types of pheromones, including alarm pheromones and food-trail pheromones, are emitted in different animal species. I wish my sex pheromones came with built-in sex-*alarm* pheromones to help weed out the bullshit early on. But pheromonal attraction isn't fatal attraction. All of us can have a pheromonal reaction without taking any action. It seems, at this point, we still have a choice.

Horror-monal hell begins once a woman has sex, and we produce something called oxytocin (not to be confused with oxycontin or oxymoron), sometimes referred to as the "bonding" or "love" hormone, which prompts deep and caring feelings for our partner. Apparently, the more sex a woman has, the deeper the bind . . . I mean, bond. Oxytocin is released during orgasm, which is why it's known as the "other big O." (It's also released during childbirth, and although I have never had children, I can only imagine that having an orgasm and giving birth are two very different experiences.)

Oxytocin explains *a lot*. Like when you meet a man, and he seems okay. You are attracted to each other, and you start to date and enjoy each other's company, but life goes on. You have sex with him, and, suddenly, BAM, you can't live without him. Is it love or oxytocin? Studies have compared the "falling in love" feeling to mental illness, including obsessive-compulsive disorder and the manic phase of manic depression, and researchers attribute hormones to being contributing factors. Does "crazy in love" really mean that we are addicted chemically to the sensations created in the pleasure centers of our brains, and the emotion is caused more by hormones than the person with whom we supposedly are in love? Are my various hormone levels what is really driving my dating and mating behavior?

And let's not forget about dopamine. Last night, I met a filmmaker, Mark Decena, who wrote and directed *Dopamine,* whose concept is "Love—real or just a chemical reaction?" Dopamine, a hormone involved in the creation of adrenaline in our bodies, is released in spades when we exercise vigorously and/or we make out with someone. This frisky neurotransmitter defines the pleasure pathways in the brain and is the hormonal equivalent of a DJ who gets the whole party started.

Maybe I'm just addicted to dopamine and/or adrenaline, and my problem is that I don't have a chemical exit strategy, other than to find something else that produces more adrenaline. Why can't I just be one of those people who enjoy skydiving or helicopter-skiing or some other emotionally safe sport to get their hormonal fix? Why do I have to continue to try to get, and stay, high on extreme love, the most dangerous sport of all?

I used to think that I had an attachment problem, because I'm good at getting into relationships and not so good at getting out when I know that the relationships aren't working. My friend Paul pointed out that I don't have an attachment problem, I have a *detachment* problem, as most of the men with whom I become involved are so inappropriate or unavailable that I eventually must leave or be left. I hate that part. Once I have sex with a man, I'm in trouble. And if the sex is really good, I'm a goner. Maybe this is where the parallel between orgasms and childbirth comes in. Both involve pain, sooner or later.

I suppose what I should have been asking myself is, Where did I get the idea that I ever should become sexually involved with anyone whom I don't consider to have serious relationship potential? Is it because I'm horny or just haven't found "the one" yet? Perhaps, as my friend Diane suggests, my "prince picker" is broken, and I just keep falling in love with the wrong kind of man.

I tend to think it's because I was raised in the seventies in the San Francisco Bay Area, where, as a little girl, I was exposed to the drug-induced "free love" era, in which sex, drugs, and rock 'n' roll ruled. Even in the suburbs where I grew up, everyone seemed to be getting naked in hot tubs and throwing keys in a bowl (couple-swapping). Whose idea was that, anyway? Surely a man's! Didn't women in the seventies experience attachment with their sexual partners? And why is it that the female of our species gets stuck with the bonding hormone, while the male gets testosterone, the "spread your seed far and wide" hormone? Somehow this doesn't seem fair. Maybe this is why women are known as the stronger sex. We have to be, in order to play the biological cards that we've been dealt.

With these last questions in mind, I dug a little deeper and discovered that men secrete the hormone vasopressin when they have sex. The theory is that the difference between monogamous and promiscuous men may have to do with how much of this hormone is released and the man's ability to respond to it. Men also secrete oxytocin, but, apparently, testosterone tends to cancel out oxytocin's effects. Studies indicate that, without oxytocin, there is no social memory. Genetically engineered mice lacking the gene for oxytocin (called oxytocin-knockout mice) seem to perform normally in every way, save one: They have complete social amnesia. These mice can't recognize or remember anyone. So the levels of oxytocin in relationship to testosterone theoretically may indicate a man's ability to differentiate one female from another. Yikes!

My friend Mark commented, "Is that why I used to roll over in the morning and never know the name of the girl I was with?" I pointed out that it probably had more to do with the quart of vodka that he'd drunk the night before, but, yes, that was the general idea.

Wouldn't it be great if, when you first had sex with a man, you could test him to determine his vasopressin, testosterone, and oxytocin production and receptivity as a predictor of his future behavior? Forget about calling psychics or your girl-friends or studying relationship-advice books like *Men Are from Mars, Women Are from Venus,* trying to interpret his bizarre male behavior. Just "accidentally" prick his finger (vs. finger-ing his prick) during sex, excuse yourself, go to the bathroom, and run some quick diagnostics. Nope, I need a minimum level of 2.0 vasopressin production combined with a two-to-one ratio of oxytocin to proceed with this man. Or, perhaps barring the ability to be that logical, be able to take some kind of emo-tional morning-after pill, an oxytocin antidote that would mit-igate the hormonal-driven desire to pair-bond with that apparently inappropriate candidate for a long-term mate.

This is assuming that you want a monogamous man. If I really like a man, I don't want him to be dating anyone else; certainly after having sex with him, I don't want him to be sleeping with anyone else. (Having the "dating other people" conversation, by the way, seems to be the fastest way to bring a hot, budding romance to a screeching halt.) I really want to be wanted and figure that if he really wants me, why would he want someone else? I am clearly *not* polyamorous. Maybe that's why I'm a serial mater, because I intuitively know that the only way to have a monogamous relationship is to keep the relationships short. I read that only three percent of mammals are monogamous, and although man (and I'm including woman in this category) is supposedly one of them, in the animal world, monogamous is defined not as having only one sexual partner, just having one lifelong mate with occasional indiscretions. (Except, of course, for Mr. Anglerfish, who is terminally faithful.) It seems like we live so much longer than most mammals. Are humans really meant to mate for life?

My romantic relationships seem to last no more than five years. When I mentioned this to my friend Chris, he told me about a *New York Times* article he read a few years ago about an anthropological study on why this might be.

"Children are somewhat self-sufficient by the time they are around five years old," he said, "so the theory is that once the offspring can more or less fend for themselves, the male will move on to plow new fields."

Nice, I thought. "Did they actually use the expression 'plow new fields'?" I asked. "Is that a scientific term?"

"You know what I mean," he said. And I do. But is it just men who are biologically programmed to mate in five-year cycles?

When I first met my ex-husband, Ted, I was in my early thirties, two years sober, suffering from depression and low self-esteem, having recently been dumped by a much younger guy on whom I still had a huge crush, working at a job that I didn't really like, and wondering when my surreal life was going to end and my *real* life was going to begin. I was quite the catch. At first glance, I thought that Ted was gay, as he appeared to be gentle, polite, soft-spoken, very successful in business, financially stable, and available. In other words, not someone I would normally date.

When he called to ask me out, I was so surprised that I turned to my roommate at the time, Leslie, and mouthed, "He wants to go out to dinner with me?" Leslie nodded her head so emphatically that I thought perhaps she knew something that I didn't, and I agreed to go. (Afterward, I found out that she had misunderstood and thought I said, "Want to go out to dinner with me?" and she was hungry, but the damage was done.)

Ted proceeded to sweep me off my feet. I didn't even know that I had a Cinderella fantasy until I found myself wearing those damn glass slippers. (Have you ever tried actually walking in glass slippers? It's tricky.) He put on a full-court press to win me over. He called me every day, gave me a new piece of jewelry each month on the anniversary of our first date, took me to dinners and plays and on trips, introduced me to all his friends, and met my family. There was no ambivalence on his part whatsoever about what he wanted, and I liked that.

I wasn't crazy obsessed with him and thought this must be a good sign. That feeling of anxiety combined with excitement was how I had defined love in the past, and it never lasted. I liked that he liked me more than I liked him. It made me feel safe, as though I had control of the situation. In the months that followed, I developed feelings of love for him, and everyone in my family assured me, "He's husband material." Also, I found him to be somewhat emotionally shut down (not so unlike the men I had dated previously, after all, and very much like my father), and this felt safe and familiar, like I was never going to be required to show up emotionally. Somehow I thought this would keep me out of harm's way. I was wrong.

After just months of whirlwind dating, he proposed, in Bora Bora. My answer was yes. In retrospect, I can see that it was more my inability to say no that landed me. I had felt like a narrator, observing my fictional character's actions, and saying yes was the next line in the script. Or to quote Lily Tomlin, I felt like a figment of my own imagination. If I had been a Method actress and able to examine what was motivating my character, I would have seen that "yes" at that time really meant that my fear of taking responsibility for my own life was greater than my fear of commitment. In other words, my decision to get married was rooted in fear.

What does it mean to commit, anyway? According to *Merriam-Webster's*, it can mean: (a) to put into charge or trust: ENTRUST; (b) to place in a prison or mental institution; (c) to put into a place for disposal or safekeeping; (d) to carry into action deliberately: PERPETRATE (commit a crime).

My version of "committing" was to entrust my future to Ted, as my keeper, so that I didn't have to take responsibility for it myself. Sure, I had feelings of love for him, but I can see now that he also had many of the things that I (or my character) wanted but didn't know how to get. He was successful in business, owned his own home, traveled extensively, had money in the bank, and drove a nice car. Somewhere in the dark recesses of my mind I believed that these things would make me safe and that I could attain them through association. (A car, make me safe? What was I thinking? I mean, it's not like he owned a Volvo, for God's sake; he had a Porsche!) What I didn't understand was that what I really *needed* was the self-esteem that comes from doing the work required to attain these things, and that self-esteem was not available through osmosis, things, or marriage.

In my defense, I wasn't conscious of any of this at the time. I see my lack of awareness and my inability to be honest with myself as the biggest problems. If I had been conscious of what was driving me, at least I could have been honest with myself and, possibly, Ted. Or maybe it's the other way around: If I had been honest with myself, I would have been more conscious. Either way, marriage seems to involve negotiations, whether they are acknowledged as such or not, and I didn't know what I was bargaining for. I couldn't admit or accept the truth about my motives, because I didn't want to be perceived as insecure. I didn't want to see or be seen as "that girl" (not the Marlo Thomas kind but the needy, lost, dependent, and fearful kind!), and I worked very hard at appearing *not* to be her, mostly to myself. As such, I wasn't in a good position to bargain. Not surprisingly, I always felt contempt for women who married for money and security, but at the time I couldn't recognize that my contempt for "those women" was my contempt for myself.

Looking back on my real motives and what I expected from my husband, instead of "Love, honor, and obey, till death do us part," the wedding vows that I should have written for us would have been more like:

I, Ted, will "keep" Wendy, read her mind, help shape and define her, support her financially (although I will always make her ask for money), and magically infuse her with self-esteem and a purpose in life.

I, Wendy, consign my power of emotional attorney to Ted. I pledge to relinquish all responsibility for my actions and commit myself to his plan of action. I promise to eventually blame Ted for my ultimate dissatisfaction, disappointment, and fear-based decision making and leave him under false pretenses (are there any other kind?).

I didn't commit to a marriage as much as I *committed* a marriage.

I became a kept woman with a big diamond ring and proceeded to morph into the suburban housewife I thought I should be, as I was absorbed into Ted's life. I started shopping at Talbot's and traded in my black leather jacket and motorcycle boots for Chanel blazers, patent-leather Cole Haan loafers, and thick snakeskin headbands. I dutifully attended award banquets, charity fund-raisers, the symphony and opera, and socialized with Ted's business partners. I feng-shuied the whole house, learned to bake the perfect brownie, and became obsessed with duvet covers. I would buy them and return them, buy them and return them, as if having the perfect duvet cover would somehow initiate happiness. (Leslie claimed that I was acting out bulimically with bedding.) I was Bree Van De Kamp in *Desperate Housewives.* My father informed me that I had "landed well."

Ted played his part, too. We were never really able to connect intimately on a deep emotional level. This was too scary for me and seemingly not a requirement for him. After a few years, Ted spent most of his time either playing golf or working. I've heard it said that there can be no intimacy without commitment, but, clearly, commitment doesn't guarantee intimacy. In the evening he would fall asleep to *Law & Order* in one room, and I would sob to Lifetime television in another, and although we ended up in the same bed each night, we were worlds apart. It felt awful to be living with someone yet feel so alone. I was afraid to talk about how I was feeling and what was really going on. When I did try to broach the subject of our inability to bridge this gap and my (our) growing unhappiness, he would reply, "If it's not a problem for me, it's not a problem." (This was very familiar. My father's approach to emotional problem solving was, if you ignore something long enough, it will eventually go away—and I did.) When I became upset or angry, Ted would retreat further into his work, saying, "We will discuss this later when you are better able to control your emotions." I never was. We never did.

As Ted and I were unable to communicate with each other, our cat became the emotional barometer in our household. The one thing I had been able to negotiate was having a cat. "We aren't getting married if I can't have a cat," I told Ted as I drove him to the SPCA several weeks before our wedding. Ted hadn't wanted a pet, felt that it was an intrusion of our privacy, but reluctantly agreed. Arriving at the kennel, we walked along the rows of cages until I stopped in front of Berkeley, a spunky young gray tabby with big green eyes. "Here he is," I said. "Here's our cat."

Shortly after our marriage, I stopped working full time, and Berkeley became my constant companion. He loved to be picked up and thrown around my shoulders, and I trained him to run up the front of my body and into my arms. Berkeley was more like a dog than a cat, and among other things, he learned to play hide-and-seek, fetch, and accompany me on walks. Sometimes he would hide in the trees overhanging our front door and drop onto my shoulders, and I would shriek and then hug him tight, laughing. Berkeley quickly became the heart of our new home.

Ted eventually fell in love with Berkeley but wouldn't let him sleep in bed with us. I would lie in bed at night listening as Berkeley cried to be let in. This turned out to be a metaphor for our marriage. Some people stay in a marriage for the children, but I felt like I stayed in my marriage for our cat. The farther apart Ted and I got, the more Berkeley would act out. When he would pee on Ted's side of the bed, I felt vindicated. When he would pee on my chair in the kitchen, I felt ashamed.

I started acting out, too, in little ways. Ted didn't want any junk food in the house, forbade smoking cigarettes, and didn't like pop music, so I kept Oreos hidden in a brown paper bag under the seat of my car, and cigarettes in my glove compartment. I started driving to a nearby shopping mall to sit in my car in the parking lot, listening to pop music, eating Oreos, and smoking cigarettes. Just like I did when I was a teenager. Ted was also a vegetarian, and because he strongly disapproved of my eating meat, I started ordering things like liver and onions or baby back ribs each time we went out for dinner.

I stopped going to AA meetings, stopped practicing any kind

of program of recovery, lost touch with all my friends, and slowly but surely started to hate my husband. Inevitably, our sex life suffered. Sharon Stone said, "Women may fake orgasms, but men fake whole relationships." I was doing both. In a small act of rebellion, I held on to my maiden name for three years. My initials were WAM, and my married initials would be WAG. I didn't like the implications, but not changing my name didn't keep me from losing my identity. (Although could I really lose something that I never really had other than in relation to someone else?)

By the time I finally changed my name, I was pregnant, and the reality of my life started to set in. I felt like I had abruptly woken up out of a prolonged boyfriend blackout, married and "with child." All the veils of denial about what I was doing were ripped away, and suddenly I wasn't living someone else's life anymore. I realized that this was *my* life, and I started panicking. I was going to be someone's *mother*. This was *really happening*. I was plagued with nightmares of dead newborn babies, crippled kittens, and being chased, always trying to outdistance some grave, imminent danger. I would awaken seeped in dread.

I thought of Ypsy, the horse I'd owned when I was a teenager. Ypsy was a beautiful black Arabian but a high-strung animal (having been broken and abused by cowboys) who was hard to catch and couldn't be tied up for long. As soon as she jerked her head and felt the rope pull, she'd realize she was tied to a fence and would start freaking out. She'd rear up and paw the fence and get all tangled up with the rope until either she was bound so tightly that she couldn't move or she managed to break free and run away.

After four months, I had a miscarriage. I was told I'd had a molar pregnancy, a genetic error that only mimics pregnancy. The sperm fertilizes an empty egg and, instead of a fetus, creates a mass of abnormal tissue, or a defective embryo is created but quickly overcome by an abnormal placenta (the organ inside the uterus that the tiny human seed depends upon for food and oxygen through the umbilical cord). I felt both ashamed and relieved. Both options seemed fitting: a pretend baby for a pretender; a damaged spark snuffed out by disease. A few months later, I simply gave up on my marriage. I felt like a bird that had been beating its wings against a glass wall, trying to get inside, until it finally stopped and dropped to the ground. A chick that had failed to peck its way out of the shell. I started pulling away from Ted, but at the same time was terrified of losing him.

"I just need to separate for a while," I said. "I need to decide what Wendy wants." I didn't want to be the bad guy. I didn't want him to hate me. I didn't want to see myself through his eyes.

"That is the kind of thing that I would say when I was trying to ease out of a relationship," he said. "I hope this isn't what you are doing, or I'll be really mad." He was scared now, and he was right. I wanted him to be there for me, to be my friend, but he said, "If you don't want to be my wife, I don't want you in my life." I knew he meant this. I let him believe that I might come back, until I was far enough away not to feel the repercussions of his pain. My bulimia flared up again, and I started bingeing and purging periodically. Although I had been clean and sober for seven years at this point, I was probably as close as I have ever been to relapsing with alcohol and drugs. Instead, I engaged in an inappropriate flirtation to keep my pain at bay.

I remember the look in Ted's eyes when I told him that I wasn't coming back. It is a look that I have seen in my own eyes many times since: betrayal. It was a cold night in San Francisco, and we had gone to dinner at Bix, ironically the scene of our first date. He tried to keep the conversation light. It was excruciating, knowing that I would break his heart. He walked me back to my car, and I told him that it was over. I could register the pain in his eyes for only a moment; it was too much for me to bear. He started crying and turned to leave, and I can still see him walking away into the foggy night, hugging himself against the cold. I didn't know who I was, in or out of the marriage. I couldn't tell him the truth—I didn't know the truth—and eventually I just couldn't sustain the illusion of who I thought I needed to be. So I broke free and ran.

We had been married for five years.

Shortly after I moved out, I met Calico, a gorgeous black, white, and brown stray cat. When Calico first appeared, I couldn't handle the idea of the responsibility of another animal, so I initially tried to ignore her. I had left Berkeley with Ted, out of guilt, and I was heartbroken. But when this skinny, beautiful, hungry, anxious Calico kept asking to be fed, I finally just had to feed her. She eventually worked her way into my house, but she was very skittish, and if she didn't have an escape hatch, like an open window, she would freak out and throw herself against the glass. She didn't seem to want to leave, she just needed to know that she could. She always seemed to be running away from something and would race down the driveway, looking over her shoulder at some phantom enemy. I could relate.

She was (and is) the craziest cat ever, but I just loved her. Still, I couldn't make the commitment to claim her as *my* cat. I told myself that she was just some stray that was going to leave soon and not to get too attached to her.

Eventually I took her to the vet, because I found she had tapeworms. The vet, Dieter, asked, "How long have you had your cat?"

"Oh, she's not my cat," I said quickly. "She's just a stray that I take care of sometimes."

Dieter looked at me sternly. "This breed of cat usually only bonds with one person in its lifetime, and they choose that person carefully. Tell me, where does Calico sleep?"

"Um, well, she sleeps on my bed, but . . ."

Dieter (who was *very* Germanic) tried unsuccessfully to hide his contempt for my ignorance and slowly and deliberately said, "Wendy, *she's your cat.*"

And just like that, I had a cat. Or, rather, just like that, I was forced to acknowledge what was already true.

Could this still be my dilemma? That I'm unable to acknowledge the truth about my motives and prefer to live in my illusions? Is this the well from which my pain is drawn? Or maybe I have yet to claim myself.

"Your problem is that you are getting exactly what you ask for, and yet you can't enjoy it!" Paul stated flatly when I asked him to weigh in on the commitment issue. "You meet some guy, Henry, Howard, Herbert, whoever, and you like him, and he's crazy about you. And, after a while, you are conflicted, because you don't really want to form a lasting relationship with him, but you *tell* yourself that you do, so then you construct a faux relationship. You have the idea that you should be mating for life, but that is *not* what you really want. You aren't dealing with the fact that you don't want more, or you wouldn't have been with these guys to begin with. When you really want something more, you will have it. In the meantime, please be less hard on yourself, and try to enjoy it. Promise me! You have no shortage of people who love you."

This was coming from the most commitment-phobic man in Hollywood, who, now in his late fifties, is still dating twenty-five-year-olds and feeling guilty about it. (Although he claims that in order to be a commitment-phobe you actually have to be willing to be involved with someone in order *not* to make a commitment.) I guess we all teach what we most need to learn, but I'm getting him a T-shirt made that says "Take my advice—

I'm not using it!" (Come to think of it, I should get one for my-self.) I suppose it's like in AA. Alcoholics know how to talk to one another because they are speaking from shared experi-ence, and Paul was certainly experienced in the dating drive-by. We dated for about five minutes.

The first time we had sex, I got a yeast infection. The night after our second time, he had a dream that his now long-dead Jewish mother was alive. He had picked his mom up in his car and inquired, "Is Wendy still at the house?" In response, she reached across his stick shift from the passenger's seat and grabbed his balls in a vise grip of death that caused him to wake up screaming. The third time we slept together, after see-ing the movie *Fahrenheit 911*, I dreamed that he had four penises intermingled with rockets, and as he was trying to in-sert this weapon of mass destruction into me, I woke up yelling, "No!" My sister Christina claims this makes us uniquely suited for each other, but shortly after that we became "just friends."

But was he right? What was so bad about my reality that I have to continue to live in fantasy? Am I really looking for a long-term relationship or just telling myself that, because I think that's what I should want? Are my actions biologically motivated or unconsciously driven by my past? Am I afraid of love? Or is five years just the statute of limitations on relation-ships? I just don't know.

I wonder if the male anglerfish has any awareness that he's es-sentially ending his life (while fulfilling his purpose) as he's mak-ing that last run into the side of the female? Does he go into it thinking that he's just "hooking up" for a good time and then he's out of there, or is he simply blindly driven by his instincts without any choice? Does it feel good to him? Maybe that's the difference between the anglerfish and me. Awareness and choice.

My therapist would say that I'm re-creating the childhood dynamics of abandonment and betrayal that were established with my mentally ill mother and emotionally unavailable father, in order to try and achieve mastery over my past. She also assures me that I don't have any experience being in healthy relationships with men, and that as my boundaries improve and my awareness increases, I will learn to better take care of myself. That I naturally will desire a "healthier" and more meaningful long-term connection.

Maybe it's like eating healthy food. Once I get into the habit of eating a carrot when I want something sweet, instead of, say, a piece of sheet cake, then I won't want the sheet cake anymore; I will *want* the carrot. I wonder what it would feel like to want what's good for me?

I guess my only question now is, Can I have my carrot and eat it, too?

CHICKS & DICKS

did you ever wonder how men pee when they have an erection? One night years ago when I was married, Ted got up in the wee hours of the morning, and I lay in bed half-listening to him moving around in the bathroom. He was in there for a long time.

"What are you doing?" I finally asked.

"Trying to pee in the bathtub," he replied.

"Why are you peeing in the bathtub?" I said.

"Because I have an erection. I can't aim into the toilet when I have an erection," he said.

I didn't know how to respond, and since I was tired and didn't feel like pursuing the erection aspect of the conversation, I let it drop (as did he). But afterward, I lay awake for a while, thinking about what men do in the bathroom. Why can't they pee in the toilet with an erection? Can't they wrestle it down into submission? And what was this peeing in the bathtub all about? You can't flush a bathtub, and if men are using the bathtub as a toilet, then what's to prevent them from peeing in the sink? Where does it end?

About that same time, I heard Madonna talking on *David Letterman* one night about how men pee while taking a shower to help prevent athlete's foot, and although I don't doubt her for a minute—this seems exactly like the kind of thing that Madonna would know (or at least the Madonna of the Dennis Rodman era)—I wondered, Where do men learn this? Is this the kind of thing they are teaching little boys in gym class?

I come from a family of four girls, and Ken dolls were my only anatomical clues about little-boy privates. (Case in point: It was almost a year after I got married before I realized that my husband was uncircumcised. I guess I had never been with an uncircumcised man before. I knew there was something different about his penis; I just couldn't quite put my finger on what it was. It's not as though I hadn't had sex before I got married, it was just that (a) I was drunk most of the time, and (b) most of the time I was drunk.)

When my sisters and I reached a certain age, my mother started herding us off from our father. The idea of him possibly seeing us naked or, even worse, us possibly seeing him naked was, for whatever reason, to be avoided at all costs. It was the five of us against the one of him. In retrospect, this tells me much more about my mother than anything else, but the result for me was modesty at all costs.

I was embarrassed to undress in front of myself for years. Our family doctor asked our mother whether we were Catholic because I was so mortified to disrobe during my regular checkups. One year in fifth grade, I had a slumber party at my house during which all the other girls undressed and played doctor, stripping down and examining each other. I was so embarrassed and humiliated that I refused to remove my flannel PJs, and suffered from PRSD (pajama-removal stress disorder) for years.

With the help of lots of alcohol, I eventually outgrew my modesty, except when it came to public nudity. I lived in Marin County, California, in the early eighties, when everybody was stripping down and climbing, buck-ass naked, into the ubiquitous hot tub at the drop of a hat. It was considered perfectly normal social behavior, like passing the butter at the dinner table or baking cookies for a new neighbor. I didn't mind being around other people who were nude; I just couldn't comfortably be one of them, and felt like a social outcast, like everyone was thinking, "Why won't she just pass the butter already? What's the big deal?" I was fine disrobing in front of, say, other women at the gym or in a trying-on-clothes situation, or with a lover one-on-one, but in front of groups of men? No. I was a prude nude. I thought this meant that there was something wrong with me, and I felt very uncool, very provincial.

The world seemed to be divided into two distinct categories: people who could happily bare all with strangers and hop into boiling water, and those who could not. (People who would pass the butter, and people who would not.) Being what I considered an uptight and repressed member of the latter group, I yearned to be a carefree and uninhibited member of the former.

Back then, I looked like a mellow California granola-eating, long-blond-hair-parted-down-the-middle, moon-and-star-wearing flower child who would have no problem romping around all naked and wild. Perhaps it was the fact that I had been born in Manhattan and was a type-A New Yorker at heart that prevented this California wild child from running nekked and free. On the outside I looked like a hippie, but on the inside I was strictly business. I don't know what, if any, other factors may have contributed to my self-consciousness, or how I had come to associate certain unpleasant feelings, like guilt or shame, with nudity. Perhaps it had something to do with my father's name being Dick—who knows? But being curious about this fear-of-nudity thing, I went online to find out more.

Turns out, there is an actual phobia called, mysteriously, fear of nudity (sometimes referred to as nudophobia). It is defined as "a persistent, abnormal, and unwarranted fear of nudity" and is supposedly very common. Huh. Not in Marin County, I thought, reading on.

"Symptoms typically include shortness of breath, rapid

breathing, irregular heartbeat, sweating, nausea, and overall feelings of dread. . . ."

Wow, sounds more like falling in love to me. I wonder if there is a clinical term for fear of falling in love naked? (Probably fear of falling in love naked, or possibly eros-nudophobia.) And is nudophobia fear of your own nudity or others'? They didn't seem to specify.

The website went on to explain: "If you are living with nudity fear, what is the real cost to your health, your career or school, and to your family life? Avoiding the issue indefinitely would mean resigning yourself to living in fear, missing out on priceless life experiences big and small, living a life that is just a shadow of what it will be when the problem is gone. For anyone earning a living, the financial toll of this phobia is incalculable: lost opportunities, poor performance or grades, promotions that pass you by. Nudity fear will likely cost you tens, even hundreds of thousands of dollars over the course of your lifetime, let alone the cost to your health and quality of life. Now nudity fear can be gone for less than the price of a round-trip airline ticket!"

Boy, this is much more serious than I thought! I had no idea that I had been living in the shadow of yet another mountain of fear. But what possible cost to my career could there be unless I was a professional stripper? I wonder what kind of promotion I didn't get because I was not comfortable getting naked in public? Come to think of it, I did pass up several opportunities to get naked with various bosses, although not in a public setting. But isn't group nudity generally discouraged in the work setting, at least in the corporate world? What "baring" does exposing my naked bits, or not, have on my ability to succeed in the world? Now, I can see if I could never be nude, even with myself, how that might be problematic. Didn't I see something about this on that Fox network show *Arrested Development*? I loved that show. One of the characters, Tobias, was a "never-nude," apparently a type of nudophobia, and subsequently he always wore a pair of cut-off jeans, even in the shower. Perhaps I am a recovering never-nude and just never-knew it.

The way that I finally got over my fear of public nudity (aside from writing this book) was much simpler and cheaper than "the cost of an airline ticket." After years of either avoiding these types of situations or enduring them, I went to a retreat at Esalen in Big Sur, California, where it is standard to take group showers before running around bare-assed naked in the hot tub area. I was determined to go along with the program this time and prove to myself once and for all that I could be comfortable under these circumstances.

Fully dressed, I marched up to the communal showers with feigned confidence, ready to pretend that I was an uninhibited exhibitionist and bare all with the best of them. I had been to Esalen before, but it had always seemed so weird to me, this undressing next to some random man, a complete stranger, and then taking a shower with him. It just seemed *wrong,* but this time I was determined to get over it already, once and for all. As I swung open the door to the shower area, the first thing I saw was the naked ass of an old man sporting a midriff T-shirt and long, hairy balls that hung down to his knees, literally, as he bent over cleaning the showers. (They say that our noses and ears never stop growing, but judging by this man, neither do testicles.)

I reared back, hands to throat. I had not been prepared to be visually assaulted! I don't know what it was about that old man's balls, but right then and there I had a moment of clarity. "That's it!" I said, and spinning on my heels, I hightailed it out of there. I finally got it. It was so simple! If I was uncomfortable being nude in public, *then I just shouldn't get nude in public!* It was not something to be overcome; it was something to be accepted! I guess it took somebody else's balls for me to find my own and finally realize that it was okay *not* to get naked with strangers. (Unless, of course, I'm dating them.)

So, back to the man-peeing thing. I did a little more research, and here's what I learned. First of all, with or without an erection, men will pee anywhere because they can: at the side of the road, in cups while driving, out the window, in a sink, over the balcony, in the bushes—wherever. One of my male friends told me that men are really no different from dogs, and this type of behavior seems to support his theory. Frankly, I'm surprised that we even bother installing men's restrooms in public for all the indiscriminate outdoor peeing that seems to be going on. Then I came across a mom-invented product

called Tinkle Targets, a potty-training aid for boys that en-
courages them to stand at the potty and pee into the center of
a floating, flushable target. The problem is, all the targets have
outdoor themes, like construction sites or motorcycle races or
sports activities, subliminally encouraging little boys to pee
into the center of a tractor-trailer or tire or soccer ball. The
manufacturers might just as well include a neighborhood
theme: Pee into the middle of this swimming pool, use the family dog as target practice, or sprinkle your neighbor's hedge.
Anywhere but indoors in the center of the toilet. My friend
Sandra, who is raising two boys, claims that her guys still prefer to pee outdoors and, in spite of all her tinkle-target efforts,
"have such poor aim that I may never be a grandmother!" This
somehow led me to find a more adult version of the Tinkle
Target—a picture of a urinal shaped like a woman's lips, which
I suppose could be a viable incentive for grown men to hit their
mark and may have been specifically developed to address the
whole peeing-with-an-erection issue.

When men actually do use the indoor facilities, they often
leave the seat up. This is a good sign, however, because at least
it means that they didn't pee splashily through the seat. (Being
a recovered bulimic, I am very familiar with, and sensitive
about, splashage issues.) Some men treat peeing like a sport, a
macho challenge to test their aim: Man versus Toilet. Then
there is the rare man who prefers to sit down on the toilet to
pee, but here other issues arise, like peeing through the crack
of the seat or running the risk of having their penis touch the

water in the basin below. I don't know what the never-nudes do, perhaps just shut their eyes and hope for the best.

Before putting the whole subject to bed, it seemed only fitting to give the first Dick in my life, my father, an opportunity to have the last word on the peeing-with-an-erection question. After a moment of silent reflection, he said, "It's an age-old problem but not an old-age problem. When you are my age, you're lucky if you can pee at all!"

SIZE MATTERS

i t's simple. All men who don't have it lie about it, worry about it, and define themselves by it. Yes, it's true. All men under six feet tall lie about their height. They can't help it. And because I'm a woman over six feet tall, six feet one and three-eighths inches to be exact (I know exactly how tall I am, because measuring me seems to be part of the early ritual of all my relationships), I am a walking, talking litmus test for men. For them, my height is my defining characteristic.

Yesterday I met a man while we were standing in line at the supermarket, and he was about five-foot-seven at most, but he was utterly convinced that he was six feet tall. When men first check me out, they usually look at my face, then quickly down to my feet to see if I'm wearing heels, then back up to either my breasts or my ass, depending on their particular vantage point. This guy's eyes traveled the circuit, and ended up eye level for him, which was somewhere in the vicinity of my throat.

"Wow, I'm a good six feet, and you are sooo much taller than me," he said. "What are you, about six-foot-five?" he asked, craning his neck toward my face. "That's freakishly tall," he added, almost to himself, while considering me as though I were a different species.

"No, I'm six-foot-one," I said as sweetly as possible, choosing to round down from my full height. Looking unconvinced, he stood on his tiptoes, shook his head, and said jovially, "Looks like someone's embarrassed about their height!" Meaning me. "Yes," I replied, "*someone* is," and, patting him nicely on the shoulders with a little more force than was absolutely necessary, I gathered my groceries to leave. "Hey, did you ever play professional basketball?" he shouted after me as I walked away. This is a typical moment in the day of a freakishly tall woman.

I know, cry me a river, but trust me, it's not as glamorous as it might seem. It's a whole different climate up here, and every once in a while, someone will still ask me, "How's the weather up there?" I know that, with all the strife in the world, freakishly tall blondes hardly sounds like a cause worth rallying around the flag about, but let me vent for a minute. It's lonely up here!

Apparently, men are curious about really tall women. After one of my first boyfriends made love to me years ago, he looked deeply into my eyes and said, "I'm so relieved. When I first met you, I thought, you know, big girl, big vagina, but that doesn't seem to be the case." "Thanks," I said, feeling both mortified and somehow grateful. It had never occurred to me that men thought that I would have a two-car garage down there just because I was tall.

I was born a relatively normal size but almost immediately started growing at an alarming rate. Within a few months of my birth, my parents had to cut a hole in the end of my baby buggy and rig a little awning to cover my rapidly extending legs. By the time I was ten, I had already surpassed my mother (five-feet-four) in height. When I was thirteen, I grew six inches in eight months, and my parents rushed me to the doctor and asked him to "make her stop!" Apparently there was nothing the doctor could do.

My childhood nicknames were Stork and Beanpole, and I always felt hugely self-conscious in the back row of my class pictures, like a middle toe that was freakishly longer than all the rest. Shopping for pants was always an ordeal, and "floods" (pants that were too short) became known as "Merrill pants" around the elementary school campus. My awkward teenage stage lasted well into my twenties, and my perception of myself as this tall, gawkward (gawky + awkward) girl still surfaces from time to time. Some of my friends still think it's amusing to call me Stretch. I am constantly hunching down to hear people at parties, and if I wear heels, well, forget about it, I'm all alone. Except, of course, for the occasional freakishly tall man who floats through my air space, usually with his five-foot-two wife in tow. (Why is it that all the really short women seem to end up with all the really tall men, including my mom, who was five-four, while my dad was six-one?)

Lots of women over the years have come up to me and said, "I wish that I had your height!" Why, ladies, why? So you can drastically diminish your odds of finding a mate taller than you? Only 2.7 percent of all men in the United States are six-four or over, and 14.5 percent are six feet or over. When I do the math, my odds aren't good. Maybe we just always want what we don't have. I always have envied curvy little brunettes, especially when it seems like they were the ones who ended up with the men over six feet. Okay, poor me, I'm done venting!

On the plus side, I can always see above everyone's head in a crowd.

It's not like I don't have sympathy for shorter men. Studies show that there is a direct correlation between height and successful men (specifically CEOs and presidents in the United States), so I'm sure that there is a lot of pressure on the below-average-height male to succeed. I wonder if this is why there are so many short leading men in Hollywood (and by my standards, short is anyone under six feet tall). Tom Cruise, Matthew McConaughey, Antonio Banderas, Kevin Costner, Jack Black, Al Pacino, Dustin Hoffman, Johnny Depp, Richard Gere, Colin Farrell, George Clooney, Leonardo DiCaprio. Seriously, these guys are short short short short short. I think Tom Cruise is about five-six, but I'm sure his bio claims six feet. Even the supposedly "tall" Brad Pitt is only five-eleven, although, according to celebrityheights.com (yes, there is a whole website that talks about this), he and Tom both wear shoe lifts. Maybe it's the Napoleon complex—the need to over-compensate for an inferiority complex about their height—that drives these men to be larger than life on the silver screen. I wonder what the opposite of that would be for me? An inferiority complex and desire to overcompensate based on being too tall and trying to appear smaller? The Olive Oyl complex?

"I just want to lie next to a man and be able to look into his eyes and play footsies at the same time," I said to my friend Kaye on a recent shoe-shopping expedition. "I want to wear heels and not tower over my date," I continued. "Does this make me shallow? Is that too much to ask?"

"So what if it does!" she replied. "If that's how you feel, then that's how you feel, and if you don't admit that, well, that just makes you dishonest. Which would you rather be?"

"Shallow or dishonest? These are my choices?" I said as I shoved my size 11 feet into a pair of darling size 10 boots. I stood up and walked around, wincing.

Kaye watched me trying to walk. "Listen, honey," she said, "if those boots are pinching your feet now, they are going to be pinching your feet six months from now." She elaborated, "Feet don't get smaller, and men don't get bigger. It seems to me that you just need to decide what you want in a man, and quit settling for what you don't want. Same with shoes."

My inability to see the forest for the sleaze with tall men may have something to do with my shoe size. Size 11 has always been a hard size to find, so whenever I would come across shoes even close to fitting me, I would buy them, just to have them. I would end up with a dozen pairs that were either too small, beautiful but badly made and so fell apart quickly, or just plain ugly. I wouldn't actually be able to wear most of them, yet I couldn't part with them, instead clinging to the vain hope that someday, somehow, they would magically fit. After years of doing this, I finally realized that even though those four-inch heels look sexy when I'm standing in front of the mirror, as soon as I try to walk, I will take a tumble, and for me, it's a long way to the floor.

I'm trying to stop buying shoes for a lifestyle that I don't have and accept that, no matter what I tell myself, I will never be able to wear a size 10 shoe. Every once in a while, I relapse, and try to jam my feet into the wrong size, usually because the shoes are either beautiful or on sale, before acknowledging that they just don't fit. I am learning how to put them back in their boxes and walk (instead of hobble) away. I am slowly becoming a discerning shoe-shopper who is willing to wait for the right ones and doesn't make as many impulse purchases. And once I do find just the right pair, I'm actually able to wear them. Suddenly I find that I'm no longer always aware of my feet. I'm able to walk without pain and get where I'm going. As a result, I have fewer shoes, they get worn a lot, and I love them all. Could this same strategy work with men?

Oddly, sometimes the very shortest of men, perhaps the

ones who feel that associating with tall women will somehow make them taller, hit on me.

When I was about ten years old, I was a *huge* fan of the pop group the Monkees. All my older cousins were Beatles fans and gave me a hard time, saying that the Monkees weren't a real band, they were just a manufactured studio group who didn't even write their own music, but I didn't care. I was *in love* with Davy Jones. He was my very first crush. I had a Davy Jones poster in my bedroom, and I dreamed of one day meeting him. I looked forward to watching their television show every week and would sing along with their theme song.

Fast-forward eight years, and I'm a freshman at Cal Poly State University in San Luis Obispo. I live in a house with four other students, including Karen, who was a reporter for the school newspaper, *The Mustang.* One day she burst through the front door shouting, "Look, the Monkees are coming to San Luis Obispo this weekend on a comeback tour!" and waving the local paper over her head excitedly. Karen had big Farrah Fawcett hair, complete with bangs curled away from her face. She was petite, buxom, and pretty—everything I felt that I was not. She was outgoing and fearless, and although I admired her, she scared me.

Apparently, the Monkees had saved Karen's life as a child. She had no father and some horrible mother who focused all her attention on the dozens of stray cats that she kept in the house, so Karen spent most of her childhood locked in her room obsessively playing Monkees records and counting the days until she was old enough to leave. She had me beat in the Monkees fan department!

"Come with me," she said, grabbing my arm. "I have a press pass, and we can get backstage." At eighteen years old, I had never been "backstage" before, and I was shy.

"I don't know, Karen," I said. "I don't want to feel like some groupie," trying to play it cool but secretly dying to meet Davy Jones.

"You won't. I am a *reporter,*" she said, and I agreed to go in her wake.

That Saturday night we went to the show. Karen was all dolled up with her big hair and her big boobs, and I felt like I always did: tall, skinny, and awkward—the sidekick ugly duckling. I was dressed in a colorful patchwork maxi skirt (floor length for those of you too young to know what this means), a purple leotard top, and clogs—very late seventies. My long blond hair was parted in the middle, and even though I was tall, on close inspection, I looked more like a frightened high school student than a freshman in college. I had trouble walking in clogs, so every ten feet or so, I would accidentally kick one off and stumble to retrieve it, while trying to pretend everything was cool. I didn't really like clogs, and they made me about six-four, but everybody was wearing them back then, and I desperately wanted to fit in.

You know how when you go back to your elementary or intermediate school as an adult, and everything looks so much smaller because you are seeing it through adult eyes? The show was like that. It was sparsely attended in a high school gymnasium, and I felt embarrassed for the Monkees. And Davy Jones was smaller than I imagined. He was only about five-two and looked like a miniature Monkee. Where was the pop idol–poster Davy Jones about whom I had dreamily fantasized when I was a child? Karen, on the other hand, didn't seem the least bit fazed by how pathetic it all seemed, and I watched her, all glassy-eyed and dreamy as though in a trance, watching them.

After the show, Karen went "backstage," which in a high school gymnasium meant the men's locker room, and introduced herself as a reporter from the school paper. I waited in the gym, too embarrassed to go with her, but after just a few minutes, she came bounding back over to me.

"They asked us to meet them at their hotel for an interview," she said. "Come on!" Dragged by the hand, I clomped out the door after her. Terrified to actually go to their hotel, I was even more terrified of what Karen would do to me if I didn't go with her. When we drove up to the motel in question, about fifteen minutes later, I was really nervous. At eighteen, I wasn't exactly in the habit of meeting men, let alone my childhood idol, in their hotel rooms. I was not one of those women who dreamed of losing their virginity to someone famous, and felt concerned that Karen might be.

The motel was a tired-looking structure built around the college to accommodate visiting parents, the equivalent of a

Motel 6. We parked and got out of the car just as the band was arriving. Karen made a beeline for Davy Jones and introduced me.

"Hi, Wendy," Davy said, checking me out from head to toe. "How are you girls tonight?"

"Fine," I stammered, and Karen pulled out her camera to take our picture.

Davy sidled up next to me, the top of his head at about my breast level, and I slipped out of my clogs and stood on my shorter leg. I had never felt taller in my life and started blushing. He put his arm around my hips and gave me a little squeeze. Karen giggled and took the picture. Micky Dolenz was there but seemed to view the whole scene with contempt and headed off to his room. Peter Tork wasn't part of this comeback tour, and neither was Michael Nesmith. I don't know what happened to Peter, but I figured that, since Michael's mother had invented Liquid Paper, he had been spared the need to re-create the magic for money.

We walked into Davy's room on the first floor. There was one queen bed, and Karen sat down and started bouncing up and down on it, her breasts and hair akimbo. She was giggling and seemed to forget why, supposedly, we were there. Davy walked over to the far side of the bed, where he retrieved a bag of granola and started munching. I was standing, with my arms folded, near the front door. I felt embarrassed to be there, like I was young and stupid, and was trying to suppress my desire to flee. This was, after all, Davy Jones, and this was my chance to fulfill a childhood fantasy.

"So, Wendy," Davy said, between mouthfuls, "how old are you?"

"I'm eighteen," I said. "How old are you?"

"You're tall," he said, ignoring my question. "I like that. And sexy," he remarked.

Huh? I thought. This was not in the script that I had in mind.

I looked at Karen. She giggled and jiggled. She seemed to have lost all of her verbal skills.

I turned back to Davy.

"In fact," he continued, swinging his granola bag back and forth and starting to walk around the bed toward me, "I'd like to climb you . . ."

He's not really going to say what I think he's going to say, is he?

"Like a . . ."

Please don't be that guy, I think.

"Monkey," he finished, and with that, sort of danced, ape-like, in my direction.

Eewww!

Karen giggled again. I glared at her.

I am mortified. I am crushed. I don't want Davy Jones to climb me like a monkey. I don't want to be climbed on. I am not a tree. Is he stoned? Surely, after all these years, he could come up with a better pick-up line than that. Clearly, he is not a song-writer. My cousins were right; they are not a real band. I was *in love* with him once, didn't he know this? Couldn't he be more sensitive to my feelings? I don't want to be a groupie. I am not cut out for this. Why me? I'm not the pretty girl; I'm the awkward, skinny, tall girl. I've never even had sex, let alone given anyone a blow job! Is this what they called monkeying around? Fortunately, my desire to flee overrode any lingering peer pressure, and I had no more time to ponder the loss of my childhood illusion.

As Davy edged around the bed in my direction, I grabbed Karen's arm and said, "Come on, let's go home, *now!*" and yanked her out of her groupie stupor and pulled her out the door.

I recently looked up Davy Jones on the Internet to see how tall he actually is. Reportedly five-three, he was also purported to have "enjoyed the novelty of going out on the town with much taller (even six-foot) women." I guess that makes me novel.

Just for fun, I went to another website where you can compare your height to that of celebrities. Apparently, I am the same height as Ashton Kutcher, Jim Carrey, and John Cusack (I wonder if he's single). Maria Sharapova was close, at six-one. Allison Janney and Elle Macpherson both measured in at six feet, and, wow, who knew that Bette Midler was five-eleven? (Oh, wait, that's five-one, sorry!) But the only women who fell into the six-foot-two category were Julia Child and Janet

Reno. Great. (Okay, I rounded my height up to six-two here, because, truth be told, I always stand on my shorter leg when my boyfriends measure me. I guess men aren't the only ones who lie!) It made me wonder, Where were all the freakishly tall leading ladies?

I love it when I meet a woman as tall as I am or, better yet, taller. It kind of reminds me of my parents' Volkswagen bus. When I was young, my parents always drove VWs, in what I considered at the time to be a pitiful and tiny rebellious act on their part to stand out amid the sea of suburban mediocrity in which we lived. VWs to them were out of the mainstream of the car world and owning one, therefore, made my parents special. I also believed that VW ownership required them to eat health food, play folk guitar, listen to classical music, and take frequent camping trips, but they still had "normal" jobs and lived in the burbs, so I don't know who they thought they were kidding. I, on the other hand, maybe because I already stood out by about a foot, wanted to blend into the Twinkie-eating, pop music–listening, motel-staying masses.

Whenever my parents spotted another VW bus on the road, especially if it was the same color as ours, they would wave excitedly and honk at the other driver, and the other driver would wave excitedly and honk back, as though they all were part of some secret underground society, with their 2.5 kids and a dog in the back. I waved, too, but felt that I was commiserating with the children in the other bus, who, I was convinced, like me, would much rather have been riding in the back of an air-conditioned station wagon with electric windows and wood-panel siding, on their way to McDonald's, instead of chewing sugar-free gum in the back of their parents' stupid hippie bus on the way to the local Co-op. But even though I hated being part of the VW tribe, at least I felt part of something.

So, when I saw all six-feet-four of Anna at a salsa dance class in San Francisco, I was thrilled. I felt like I had finally met someone from the long-lost tribe of Amazon women. I had really wanted to take this class, because I *love* to dance. Dancing makes me happy. Dancing with shorter partners in some types of dancing isn't really a problem, but with salsa, you want your partner to be the same height or taller. I was terrified of reliving my seventh-grade-dance, Susan Anton/Dudley Moore nightmare, so I had put off registering for the class as long as possible, hoping for a fabulous, tall, gay best friend who could play Rupert Everett to my Julia Roberts to show up.

After a few years, when no such gay prince appeared, I finally said, *Fuck it, just take the class.*

As the dance studio was in San Francisco, which has a large Hispanic and Asian population, I wasn't surprised when I walked in to see that most of the men were short, even by normal standards. As I surveyed the crowd, I imagined chalk lines above their heads, labeled with their estimated heights: five-nine, five-seven, uh-oh, five-four. This wasn't good. I suddenly felt a little like an amusement-park ride that nobody in the room was tall enough to board. Maybe some of these guys have that same Susan Anton/Dudley Moore fear, I thought nervously as we gathered around in a double circle to begin.

The men formed the inner circle, and the women the outer. We were to dance with one partner for two minutes and then move to the next person. Moving through the circle of men, I could see the panic start to rise in their eyes as I approached. At least we only have the same partner for two minutes before a whistle blows and we switch, I thought, gearing up to bend over backward when twirled by the latest terrified man standing in front of me. As we started to dance, the door opened, and the tallest woman I've ever seen walked into the class. I later learned that her name was Anna. She was easily six-four and gorgeous. Maybe she's a he, I thought, but after checking for an Adam's apple, realized that she was the real thing.

Just seeing her made me feel braver, and as I caught Anna's eye, we gave each other the nod. If she can do it, I thought, then so can I, and, suddenly not feeling so alone, I smiled at my little partner and leaned down to be twirled.

CO-DEMENDENCY

i met jack at the Friday night AA meeting in San Francisco, referred to informally as the "toothbrush" meeting. I always thought this meant that you should brush your teeth beforehand, as lots of attractive singles attended this meeting, and you obviously would want to have white teeth and fresh breath—like a chemically dependent Crest commercial. Turns out it meant that you might want to take your toothbrush to the meeting just in case you "got lucky." Now, perhaps I was naïve, or maybe there was a dental-health wave sweeping the nation that I was not aware of, but this concept was rather shocking to me. The idea that anyone would plan to take a toothbrush to an AA meeting, or anyplace else for that matter, hoping to "get lucky," seemed bizarre.

I may not have packed my toothbrush that night, but I got

lucky, all right. On my way out of the meeting, Jack jumped in front of me to thank me for sharing, as I had been the speaker that evening. He was movie-star handsome in that (younger) Nick Nolte, slightly-decaying-bad-boy kind of way—a Mel Gibson and Tom Berenger concoction, with a certain dented quality that made me want to trust him, like a fallen angel on a mission to regain his wings.

He was tall, wore a heavy chocolate-brown leather jacket that creaked like a saddle when he moved, his smile a Michelangelo outtake.

"Hi, my name is Jack," he said.

Yummy, I thought.

"Thanks so much for your share tonight," he continued. "I don't even know you, and I feel proud of you." And he smiled that Renaissance smile.

God, I thought, that is maybe the single best compliment I've ever received, and shyly introduced myself.

"It's a pleasure to eat you . . . I mean, *meet* you," I stammered. Damn, why did really handsome men always make me so incredibly stupid? And there was something else about him, too. What was it? He seemed familiar in a way that made me want to take him home and lick his wounds.

As I stood there staring at him, my girlfriend Jacqui stepped in and invited Jack to join us for coffee. He agreed and offered to give me a ride to the nearby Mel's Diner. As I was sitting in the front seat of his vintage BMW (such a manly man's car), he leaned across me to pull something out of the glove compartment. The leather of his jacket groaned (or was that me?), and he smelled like Mennen deodorant and saddle soap. I felt something like déjà vu, and I swooned. I went into an olfactory stupor then, and between that and the creaking leather and his killer smile, I was in sensory overload, and the hook was set.

I felt like I had hit the Jackpot.

I had recently broken up with someone I had been dating in New York. This, my first relationship after my marriage ended, had begun at the office one day when I found myself having phone sex with Timmy, a business associate I had yet to meet in person. It was as though I had been sexually re-pressed during my marriage and was suddenly shot out of an Elizabethan cannon, reborn as PhoneSexGirl, the sexy super-heroine who uses her oral skills for aural thrills. Able to leap across personal boundaries and social decorum in a single breath. In the spirit of "when she was good, she was very, very good, but when she was bad, she was better," PhoneSexGirl was one hot and horny bitch. It was like someone had thrown a match onto my gasoline-soaked libido. One minute Timmy and I were flirting a little and talking about marketing tac-tics, and the next minute I was kneeling in front of him on the crowded New York City subway train (of his mind), with his cock down my throat. It scared me, how good I was at being bad on the phone, and I briefly considered starting my own 1-900 sex-talk business, maybe calling it No Hang-ups, or Bitches Without Borders. (After all, anal sex is *soo* much eas-ier on the phone, isn't it?) Instead, I settled for acting out every fantasy I had ever had and more on the phone with Timmy. We would talk for hours each night, and during the day I would write erotica to prepare for our nightly rendezvous.

When I finally flew to New York to meet him, Timmy turned out to be around six inches shorter than me, a bit of a drunk with massive mother issues, and the reality of our sex life never came close to matching the fantasy of our phone sex. Ironically, PhoneSexGirl became *Phoney*SexGirl. Still, I had swallowed my own bait—hook, phone line, and stinker—and for me, getting the stinker back out was always easier said than done. I continued to date him for about a year, obsessively trying (as always) to reconcile fantasy with reality, until a man whom I had been in L-O-V-E with for years showed back up on the scene: my therapist, Brian. Or rather my ex-therapist. But apparently enough time had elapsed since I had been his patient (according to some code of ethics) for Brian to call me up one day and ask me out.

The first time I'd swept into Brian's office, wearing my eighties purple leather jacket, the perfect accessory for my hubris and desperation, I took one look at all six-feet-five of him and thought, Finally, the perfect man for me: tall, handsome, *and* a mental-health professional.

Unfortunately, he was married, seemingly happily, so I settled for fantasizing during our sessions about ways in which his wife could be eliminated. It's not like I wanted her to suffer. She would pass quickly and painlessly, perhaps in a freakish flash flood or from a cerebral hemorrhage, leaving the way clear for me to move in and apply my very special brand of first aid. I loved children, and he had several little girls. I would help them recover from their mother's death, and we would all live happily ever after in a glowing bubble of mental health. While I was daydreaming about his wife's demise, Brian was busy trying to apply a tourniquet to control my emotional hemorrhaging. After two months in therapy with him, my internal bleeding finally broke through, and I landed in that twenty-eight-day alcohol-and-drug-treatment facility.

After rehab I continued in therapy, and Brian helped me, maybe even saved my life. He was one of the very first people with whom I was able to be honest (except, of course, for the part about my wanting his wife dead), and after a few years of therapy we became more like friends.

"You remind me of a girl at a seventh-grade dance who really, really wants to get out on the dance floor but is too afraid to move," he'd said. He was right. I had been that frightened seventh-grade girl stuck on the sidelines of my life, and my years of therapy with Brian seemed to boil down to a Nike ad: "Just do it," he'd say. The question remained, Just do what? Or whom?

When I got married three years later, both he and his wife attended my funeral . . . I mean, my wedding. Shortly after that, his wife ended up leaving him for a woman (the perfect solution—why didn't I think of that?—but *damn,* I was a newlywed and still his patient!), and then six years later he called me.

His previous advice to "Just do it" had evolved into "Just do me," when he expressed the desire to be my "sex buddy." I wasn't familiar with this term, but I got the gist. I was dubious, conflicted, intrigued. Flattered. Repulsed. Confused. All very familiar dating sensations, but you would think that after years of unearthing and examining my issues, he would have known better. Although to be fair, there were so many different Wendys, it might have been difficult to keep track of which one he was dealing with. I was like my own disenfranchised franchise.

One holiday season I'd given him a card I made using construction paper and glitter with a child's awkward handwriting. It looked like something a parent would proudly hang on the refrigerator, featuring a big green Christmas tree decorated with multiple-colored, multiple-personality Wendy ornaments. There was sexual siren Wendy, dutiful Wendy, overly empathetic Wendy, addict Wendy (aka Sabrina), sullen and betrayed teenage Wendy, sweet adolescent Wendy, and feisty baby Wendy, and on the top of the tree was a star, with a great big question mark.

He knew me, so I thought it was possible that he knew something that I did not. Maybe he had the answer to my question.

Brian and I only went out a couple of times. It was just too weird, like I was dating my father. Or brother. Or uncle. Something. Wrong. Our ill-fated romance ended after our one and only incestuous kiss good night (*shudder*). When he slipped his tongue into my mouth, it felt illegal, and not in a good way. I viewed my inability to engage in a sexual relationship with my ex-therapist as great progress on my part and felt that I was more than prepared to engage in this new relationship with Jack.

Judging by these recent standards, Jack seemed relatively normal. We were both sober, lived in the same area code, and were the same age. He wasn't married or pining away for some other woman, didn't appear to be gay, was drop-dead gorgeous, and as far as I knew, wasn't related to me. So far, he looked like a safe bet.

I gave Jack my number at the end of the evening, and we went out the next night and just about every night after that. Our sexual chemistry sizzled, but we decided to wait awhile before acting on it. He, ostensibly because he was a fallen born-again Christian who was trying to claw his way back into the Lord's good graces, and me because, well, after my PhoneSexGirl debacle, I really wanted to try and do the right thing and be a good girl again. Act like a respectable, responsible woman (whatever that means). I, too, wanted to redeem myself.

We started hanging out. He wasn't the most articulate person I'd ever met, but sometimes words are highly overrated. And he was good at other things. Like wanting me. I liked the physicality of him. He was big and strong and beautiful, and when he held me, I felt safe. He also wanted me as a girlfriend, not just a sex buddy, and I liked that.

Jack had been a stockbroker the previous year but had fallen into a deep depression, eventually had to quit his job, and was put on a heavy-duty combination of antidepressants. He eventually went back to work, reborn as a salesman at a popular Bay Area store, purported to be *the best place to buy a mattress*.

This was not a glamorous job, but I admired the humility that it must have taken to work there, and I imagined him inflating balloons for a big holiday weekend blowout sale, tying them, one by one, to the bedposts on the display floor. In my mind's eye, I noticed that his suit was a little threadbare and that he needed new shoes. His hair, on the other hand, was perfect.

When not hawking mattresses, Jack spent his time in poker houses or online, chewing Nicorette gum, smoking cigarettes, and buying and selling stocks. He was seriously involved in something called "day trading." I didn't know anything about the stock market, but I wanted to. This was during the tech boom, when everyone around us in San Francisco was making a fortune, and Jack desperately wanted to be in on the gold rush. His enthusiasm for it was infectious, and I had not thought to be inoculated against the fever.

Now, it's not like I was completely blind. He was, after all, a *failed* stockbroker turned day-trading mattress salesman. I understood there was potential cause for concern, that there might be the outside chance that he was a gambling addict. He was, after all, a recovering alcoholic, and I knew how addiction

could migrate from one outlet to another: alcoholism to worka-
holism to sex addiction to gambling addiction to smoking to
religious fervor to chocoholism to obsessive dog breeding or
gardening or nitpicking or *whatever* one puts one's attention
to. Once an addict, always an addict. But to date I hadn't had
any experience with gambling addicts or the stock market, so
I reasoned that maybe the two could go hand in hand, in a
good way. After all, wasn't Lucifer originally an archangel? I
believed that the power of obsession could be used for good instead of just for evil. Harnessed addiction. Like solar power.
And that maybe playing the stock market was just his *passion,*
selling mattresses his "day job," and he knew what he was
doing. I wanted to think so. I wanted to be proud of him.

On the other hand, I had plenty of experience with depression, and so I empathized with Jack. I understood this
disease all too well and had dated *plenty* of medicated men before. So many, in fact, that if you were a man who was wildly
attracted to me, you were probably suffering from depression,
whether you knew it or not. Or would be soon. I called this
diagnosable dating. I was like a human antidepressant. In the
past, instead of keeping a well-stocked bar, I might just as well
have stocked my medicine cabinet with Wellbutrin or Prozac,
in the event that my boyfriends forgot their meds. I always *had*
liked to provide a full-service B&B environment the morning
after. "Bloody Mary? Coffee? Zoloft? Saving . . . I mean, shaving cream? Fresh razor blade?"

Sometimes, when reaching down into their darkness to try

to help them out, I had been pulled down instead, but I had still been drinking then, and I felt stronger now, more capable. I had been sober for a while and knew how to live with depression. I felt more than qualified to handle this situation. I wanted to see Jack succeed, wanted to help him, wanted to give him the benefit of the doubt. I wanted to be a *fucking* saint, in the nicest possible way.

"you give good bed," I teased, gazing into his frosted blue eyes as we lay on his luxurious cashmere pillow–topped king-size bed. (Dating a mattress salesman was not completely without perks.)

"Ha ha," he said, and pulled me close. We had not had sex yet, but he was good at cuddling, and lying on his bed was as advertised: like floating on a cloud.

"I had a margin call today," he said, sitting up to talk to me, serious now.

"Is that anything like a booty call?" I teased, sitting up, too, following suit.

He smiled angelically and continued, "No, margining stock is when you borrow against the market value of a stock, like taking out a second mortgage on a house, but if the stock price drops below a certain level, you have to pay the difference—the margin call—in order to stay in the game," he explained. "The market dropped today, and now I need to come up with $5K to cover my margin call," he said. He seemed worried.

"What happens if you don't come up with the money?" I asked.

"I'll have to sell a bunch of the stock. Everything that I've got is tied up in this one stock. It's my whole stake in the market."

The ex–holy roller turned high roller, I thought.

I had been making money, good money of my own, for the first time in my life, and I was proud of that. I had always had jobs, but working at the ad agency had kicked me into a whole new income bracket. As such, I happened to have extra money lying around. I really wanted him to get ahead and to be able to feel good about himself. I could see that he was struggling with his self-image, and we both wanted to be able to see him as something other than a mattress salesman. I wanted to help him, figuring that with just a little fixing up, this guy could be great!

"Why don't I lend you the money?" I offered. "The stock will come back, right?"

"It will come back, it's a rocket. But I can't take your money," he said.

"Why not? I just happen to have an extra $5,000 in my checking account. It's no big deal."

"No, I couldn't possibly."

"I insist."

"Well, okay, thanks."

Then I felt it, the rush. Like I had won the Lotto.

And just like that, we were off to the races.

His stock rose, and he paid me back, with interest. My hero. I felt like I had been able to contribute to his success, and the interaction brought us closer. I experienced a whisper of relief, like maybe now everything was going to be okay, followed, inexplicably, by a slight letdown. We carried on.

When he had another margin call a few weeks later, this time for $10,000, I didn't hesitate to give it to him. He even offered to sign an IOU. "Don't be silly," I said. It felt good to be able to bail him out, and I didn't want him to think that I didn't trust him. When I started to feel a little anxious, I looked forward to what I was sure would follow—more relief.

Weeks went by and everything was fine. We finally had sex. Suddenly everything was not fine. It was not what I expected. He was so virile looking, so confident, and so sexy, how could he be this bad in bed? He seemed conflicted, like so many ex–religious fanatics or recovering Catholics. As though his God-given sexual desire was a sin, a punishment. He couldn't enjoy it, either one: the sex or the punishment. Sometimes religious fervor combined with guilt makes the sex hot. In his case, not. Plus, multiple antidepressants did not make for multiple orgasms, and he often lost his erection and was seldom able to come without what seemed like an endless amount of jerking off. He had a strong draw, with a big bluff, but he had to fold more times than not.

He had been betting on the come, and now so was I.

His cock wasn't the only thing that was plummeting, and soon the market started crashing again. Suddenly he needed another $10,000, then $5,000 more, then $20,000, and so on. I cannot adequately explain what happened to me next, other than to say that it was like free-falling into a deep black hole without a parachute. For whatever reason, I could not bear to watch this guy fall into the darkness alone, and like some ass-backward superhero with a flashlight, I thought that jumping into the abyss after him would save him. But it wasn't really even a thought; it was more like I was overtaken by an irresistible compulsion to jump. Bungee jumping without the bungee. Like the feeling of vertigo that I always experience on a ski lift when I'm afraid that my body is just going to hurl itself off the chair into the valley below, and I will be powerless to stop it from happening. Only this time it happened, and it felt like the fear of falling somehow had caused the fall. Like I had been thrown overboard by my fear.

Intellectually, I knew that I was chasing my original investment. I was so fixated on that unrepaid $10,000. It had seemed like such a huge amount of money to me, and I now felt humiliated by the largesse of my gesture. In order to justify what I had done, I had to keep going. It was a surreal game now, and the margin calls I was meeting seemed like Monopoly money. Everything I did caused me to be farther away from where I wanted to be, like I was trying to rewind by pushing Fast Forward and I couldn't find the Pause button. I pulled money out of savings and credit lines, and margined my own stock accounts, which I had barely even looked at before. I had always experienced a lot of fear in regard to my finances, even when I had money, but this was agony without the ecstasy. Pride cometh, then goeth . . . goeth, gone.

After that free fall, the market stabilized again, and although his stocks recovered, I did not. I could hardly believe what had happened. I wanted him to sell immediately and pay me back, but he wouldn't, and I couldn't make him. I started to panic. I may have been playing hearts, but he was playing poker, and he began to raise the stakes. He still wanted to get ahead, he said, wanted to build a nest egg for the future. He doubled-down on the charm, was effusive, affectionate, demonstrating a willingness to change. "Just a little longer," he said, "just until I get my feet back on the ground." Just enough to keep me in the game. Like I had a choice.

He had apparently regained enough footing, in his mind, to buy himself a used daffodil-yellow Mercedes SL. Disbelief. How could he buy a car instead of paying me back? But I tried to stay calm and told myself, Okay, maybe *now* he will feel better about himself and be able to start showing some gratitude for "everything that I've done for him."

If you put a frog into a pot of boiling water, it will immediately hop out, but if you put that same frog in a pot of cold water, and slowly turn up the heat, it will boil to death. I was boiling.

The market fell again, and me with it. I spent my birthday that year circling the drain, running around town, pulling more money from my lines of credit and selling what was left of my stock to feed this insatiable beast. I had never been in debt before, always paid my bills on time, always paid my taxes. I didn't even like playing the slot machines. This was unthinkable to me. My stockbroker was concerned, perplexed. I told him it was a family emergency. I was frantic, terrified, embarrassed, humiliated, ashamed. The more money I shelled out, the more invested I was in getting it back, and the more I had to justify what I was doing by shelling out more. It was a giant shell game, and I was desperately trying to pretend that I was not going to lose.

Jack showed up at my house that evening with flowers, birthday presents, and compliments, and took me out in his fancy new car to an expensive dinner. All I could think was, *This evening's show is being sponsored by Wendy's, unrivaled in giving people what they want—and uncompromising in giving people what they deserve. Feed the hunger!*

Such a pretty picture. Such a *lie*!

My jackpot had turned into jack shit. And the very worst part of all was that my stock in myself was plummeting. My inability to watch him lose had cost me everything: money, self-respect, sanity. Not surprisingly, our sex life went from bad to worse.

I wanted out but was terrified that if I left I would never get my money back. I finally started getting more demanding. Under duress he signed a contract that specified exactly what he owed me, promising to repay with interest, but I felt hopeless and scared. Having a signed contract gave me about as much relief as taking an aspirin before open-heart surgery. I knew there was no way to squeeze blood from this stone. He was bloodless, and I was getting bloodthirsty.

"The most important lesson in the stock market is to learn when to cut your losses and not throw good money after bad," my gambling addict/*successful* stockbroker friend Grant (who also owned a Mercedes SL) told me when I described the situation. "Sounds like you need to cut and run," he advised.

No, my mind screamed, *no, No, NO, NOOOO!*

So I tried to be nicer, I tried getting mad, I tried bolstering Jack's ego, I tried threatening him. Nothing worked. He was impervious. I felt like I was being buried alive, desperately trying to claw my way to the surface. Only instead of digging up, I was digging down, and my grave got deeper and deeper. I had completely forgotten how to breathe, yet I was still alive. I may have been betting on the come, but I had played right into his hands.

It was a nightmare.

Why couldn't I wake up and walk away? Let the chips fall where they may? My therapist, Juliette (no more male therapists for me), had a word for it: *co-dependency.* I HATED that word. I knew what it meant, in theory; I just couldn't *comprehend* it. A co-dependent.

I didn't *want* to be a co-dependent! I was already a recovering alcoholic, wasn't that *enough*? I didn't want *any* of this to be happening. This was not something that happens to *nice* people. Oh my god, Oh My God, OH MY GOD! I was turning into one of those pathetic women on *60 Minutes* whom I had always held in contempt, who stupidly trusted her handsome, charming boyfriend who ends up being a bigamist lowlife scum-sucking *grifter*. We see her being interviewed from jail because of her complicity in his illegal affairs, and Morley Safer is asking her, "Didn't you notice that he was robbing you blind? Why won't you testify against him?" and Morley's looking at her with this fake compassion but really thinking, "You are *such* a fool!" and he's pissed that he's stuck interviewing this stupid bitch while Mike Wallace got the lead story, and she just *sits* there looking *horrible* in her orange jumpsuit and stringy blond hair with gray roots and vacant eyes, saying, "But he was so good to me and my kids. . . ."

This was unfuckingbelievable! What the hell was happening? How could this happen to *me!?* My would-be hero was a big fat zero! He wasn't even good in bed. Why couldn't I just leave?

It was time to take stock. I struggled to make sense out of crazy. I employed my intellect and my sarcasm to find a way to control my feelings, to affect the outcome. I went online to collect evidence. Like I was filing a police report. On myself.

co-dependent *adj.*
1: mutually dependent
2: of, or relating to, a relationship in which one person is psychologically dependent in an unhealthy way on someone who is addicted to a drug or self-destructive behavior, such as *chronic gambling*.

Joker poker, I thought, as I read on with growing dread.

"The co-dependent tends to take care of, with a great amount of attention, everyone else's feelings and actions, while neglecting to take care of his or her own."

Do tell.

"The co-dependent is a reactive individual instead of acting for himself or herself."

Fluffing and bluffing.

"Co-dependent personality disorder is characterized by a dysfunctional relationship with others including oneself."

Flush.

"This individual is living through someone else or for someone else and not for himself or herself."

A natural.

"Co-dependents are controlling and will blame others instead of taking responsibility. They live in a state of victimization while trying to fix others, and they will exhibit intense anxiety when it comes to intimacy."

Scolding and folding.

"Co-dependents come from dysfunctional families."

Raised crazed.

"The co-dependent personality is often a rescuer constantly trying to save others from the consequences they are about to face. They will go to great lengths to do this insofar as giving them money and lying for them if they think they are helping them. Of course, this type of rescuing only serves to keep the dysfunctional individual in that state, thus enabling the person they are rescuing to continue making the poor choices that they are experiencing."

Busted.

"The co-dependent individual is a controller and will do so by whatever means works best. The intentions of the co-dependent are well founded; they are only executed in the wrong fashion. The co-dependent needs to learn that there is only one person in this world whom any of us can control, and that would be herself or himself. Once co-dependents come to this understanding, they will then be able to help the dysfunctional people in their lives start to take responsibility for their own actions."

Pass.

Okay, *okay,* I fucking qualify already! So shoot me. I had tried to "help" him. I had mistaken this for caring about him, for him. I was mentally ill. Surprise, surprise. But this word, *co-dependent,* wasn't enough! It didn't come anywhere near describing how angry and betrayed and powerless I *felt*! My reality and my money were all mixed up with his now, and I couldn't tell whose was whose. I had started assuming his characteristics: smoking, swearing, lying to friends, going as far as developing a hiatal hernia, something from which he suffered, where your stomach protrudes into your chest cavity. I struggled to swallow. My stomach seethed. I couldn't sleep, felt the void of depression tugging, was having nightmares again, and I was SO FUCKING ANGRY! I had traded down, me for him. I had gone to the mattresses—with myself. I was going mad.

I wrote a list of "tells" that had led up to this nightmare—my own personal Twenty Questions, all the red flags that I had chosen to ignore— hoping that by identifying what I was actually doing, it would sink *in* before I sank, and I would be able to cut my losses and run.

TELLS

1. Has he recently come out of a deep depression? ✓
2. Is he on one or more antidepressants? ✓
3. Is he a recovering alcoholic and addict who doesn't work a program of recovery? ✓
4. Does he obsessively chew Nicorette gum *and* smoke cigarettes? ✓
5. Are your moods dependent upon his wins? ✓
6. Is he always fishing for compliments? ✓
7. Do you see him as a fixer-upper? ✓
8. Do you have to drag him up conversation hill? ✓
9. Are your arms tired from trying to reel him in? ✓
10. Is your jaw tired from trying to make him come? ✓
11. Do you find yourself pretending that he's a nice guy underneath it all? ✓
12. Does he remind you of anybody? ✓
13. Does he buy you gifts for your birthday with your money? ✓
14. Do you lie to your friends about what's really going on? ✓
15. Do you find him jerking off to online porn sites? ✓

16. Has he ever shared with you that he might have murdered someone in his car in a blackout and left the scene of the crime? ✓

17. Did he father a child whom he was not willing to take responsibility for? ✓

18. Are you afraid to hurt HIS feelings? ✓

19. Has his family basically disowned him, and when they meet you look at you like you are crazy? ✓

20. Do you want to leave him but feel like you are STUCK? ✓✓

I reviewed the list. I passed the test. A perfect score. Look, Wendy. LOOK. *Can't you see?* I could see, all right. There was just one word for my state of being right now:

co-demendent *adj.* 1: Super Glued to a jackass 2: see above

The scary part was I really could see, intellectually, what I had done, but I still couldn't get loose. It was as though I didn't have a choice. I just couldn't *help* it, and that was my biggest tell of all: that I was addicted to the addict. I was gambling on a gambler. I was chasing the uncatchable. The undesirable. The dragon. I needed relief. I needed answers. But what was I supposed to do now?!

I resorted to prayer.

And then Al-Anon.

I am sitting in an Al-Anon meeting. I notice that I hate everyone around me. Plastic smiles, endless rules, and laminated readings. I'm in so much pain, I have NO idea how to talk about it, and I can barely listen. The speaker is sharing now about the three A's of Al-Anon: Awareness, Acceptance, and Action. I despise her. Her hair is perfectly coiffed. She is wearing pearls. I'm *sure* they are fake. FUCK these people, I think. What is all this Pollyanna-fucking-bullshit! A heavy-rock station is blaring in my head, so loudly that I almost miss the quieter voice that whispers, *Whatever you put your attention to rules your life.* I *hate* this little voice right now, so like an angry teenager, I crank up my black-metal mentally ill music and focus all my attention on *my* version of the three A's: Agitate! Accept Nothing! Act Out! Okay, three A's, one N, and an O. (*Doesn't that spell NO, Wendy?* says the quiet voice, gently mocking me, trying to get my attention and make me smile.) The blaring gets louder in response until my head feels like it's going to blow a fuse. FUCK IT, I think, shorting out. Al-Anon is helping about as much as putting a Band-Aid on a gushing artery, and I slam out of the meeting.

I knew I was in trouble, but the anger made me feel powerful. Damage control. I knew I had put myself in harm's way, but I was afraid. Afraid that if I left him, he would never give me my money back. Afraid of what would happen to him if he lost everything. Afraid that I couldn't save him. Afraid that I couldn't save myself. Afraid of what people would say. Afraid to let go. Afraid to hold on. I couldn't quite leave, but I couldn't stay much longer, so I waited. For what, I did not know.

I struggled over the coming weeks to manage my feelings and hope for the best. Dread accompanied me everywhere, like a Katie Holmes Scientologist bodyguard. I couldn't shake it. Each time I had the impulse to pick up the phone and scream at Jack, as though there was something that I could say that would change anything, I resisted. It didn't help. Nothing helped. My AA sponsor told me to equate picking up the phone to call Jack with picking up a drink, and to get down on my knees and pray for guidance instead. I could remember that. I knew what it meant for me to drink. So I waited. It was like waiting for death.

Finally, more margin calls, but this time I couldn't meet them. I had maxed out all my accounts and was deeply in debt now, both financially and emotionally. I had nothing left to give. I was hollow, metallic. I felt karmically cursed, as though I had been a slave trader in a past life. When was I ever going to be debt freed? I had been hemorrhaging emotionally for years. It had taken bleeding money to get my attention. There was to be no resolution here, only dissolution. This ex-stockbroker had broken me. The smell of saddle soap and Mennen deodorant had cost me a fortune. My $100,000 olfactory mis-stake. I had no cents. I was going to the poor-me house.

Prayer did little to relieve my suffering but brought clarity instead. *Whatever you put your attention to rules your life.* I could listen now: *Awareness, Acceptance, Action.* I could see that I was never going to get him to buy into my version of our story. I could never make him see what *he* had done, never make *him* take responsibility for it. There was only me: what I had done, accepting the consequences of my actions, not endorsing but accepting. It was very simple and impossibly hard. It sucked. I had been holding on tightly while desperately trying to let go. I was an oxymoron. I had gone for broke and I had gotten there. Now I needed to leave the money on the table, get up, and walk away.

Just do it.

It was Thanksgiving Day. I did not feel grateful. I was sick with fury. Seething, resentful, scared. I was still engaged in a not-so-civil war with myself, but the end was near, if not clear. We had been invited to dine with his longtime (or long-suffering) friends. When we arrived, I was introduced to their sparkly five-year-old daughter, Kate. Little girls are drawn to me, I to them, and when I was introduced to this fluffy little blond beauty, she looked up at me and simply said, "You are good," pointing to me, "and you are bad," pointing to Jack, and walked away. Just like that. Jack laughed, shrugged, but I was stunned. This little girl had just met me. She had grown up with Jack. She could say what I could not. She could speak her truth. She had called the game. She was my hero.

"This is over," I said later as we sat outside my house in his car. Verbal grenades were exploding in my head, screaming, *"He'll never pay you back now. You are such an idiot. You will lose everything. He will lose everything. If you just wait him out, everything will be okay!"* I had come to view these as the voices of the oppressor, calling out from behind enemy lines.

He looked at me, absolutely incredulous. "I thought we would get married," he said, as though he had no idea why I would say such a thing.

I stared at him. *He cannot see what he has done.* I had been dating O.J. Simpson. His reality was distorted. I could barely see myself, but even through the bloody haze of my rage and my fear, I could finally see what I had been afraid to see all along. That he was sick, really sick. Maybe dying. Maybe dead. I couldn't help him. And now I was sick again, too. But I wasn't dead, not yet, and suddenly it felt like my life was at stake. I was dying to see. I wanted to live. I had to get out.

As I opened the door of his little Mercedes death coupe, I could feel steel ripping and shearing in my mind, as though I was being extracted from this relationship with the Jaws of Life. As the twisted metal was lifted from my head, I *knew* that if I reached up for help, right then, I could be pulled from this wreckage. This was my chance. I also recognized that part of me wanted to stay, wanted to bleed to death on the beautiful cream-colored leather upholstery of his coffin. But that Wendy was not in the driver's seat anymore. At least not right now.

He grabbed my arm to stop me and smiled, lopsidedly, as though he were having a stroke.

"I'm sorry," he said, in an uncharacteristic moment of truth or, more likely, a last-ditch bluff to keep me in the game.

I paused for one last look. His smile looked different now. I noticed for the first time how yellow his teeth were, and what had seemed like laugh lines previously now resembled self-inflicted battle scars.

"I'll just bet you are," I said, and turning, reached up and pulled myself free.

BEHIND BRAS

this morning I went to San Quentin prison to play tennis. My very enthusiastic born-again Christian friend, Alex, works with a church group that brings male tennis players and a basketball team from the outside world into prisons to play with the inmates who have earned that privilege, kind of a Good-versus-Evil play date, and he wanted to add a woman to the team.

"You are the only woman I know who might be willing to do this," he explained when he called to ask me to join them for an upcoming visit. "I thought it would be interesting to introduce a female tennis player into the mix to help socialize the inmates," he continued, somewhat unconvincingly.

I wasn't sure whether to take this as a compliment or an invitation to be briefly incarcerated for what I'm sure he saw as my sinful behavior (sex outside of marriage). I knew from personal experience that Alex was very creative in his efforts to convert nonbelievers, and it sounded a little like he was pimping me out for the Lord. I had nothing against Jesus himself; I just wasn't crazy about some of his groupies and had never been much of a team player. Plus, I didn't *really* play tennis, and Alex knew that. He also knew that I had recently been through the relationship mill and had subsequently been in a funk for months. No matter where I was or what I was doing, I felt as though I should be somewhere else doing something else.

In his own evangelical way, I think Alex was trying to take advantage of my malaise to hook me up with Jesus by pulling me into *his* "good works" service corps. I don't think it even occurred to him that exposing me to a male prison population as a social lubricant was just a little devilish and might not have the desired effect.

But still, I had never been to prison before, desperately needed a new perspective, and *was* curious, so in my quest to do something different, I agreed.

This wasn't the first time Alex had tried to set me up with Jesus. Several years ago he attempted to convince me that if only I would accept Jesus Christ, our Lord and Savior, into my heart the way *he* had, my troubles would be over. I told him that I had enough man troubles, thank you very much, and didn't believe that letting yet another handsome, charismatic man into my heart would solve my problems (which often seemed to stem from letting the wrong handsome, charismatic

man into my heart). Plus, I really didn't like the idea of a mas-
culine God, although, ironically, I often ended up worshipping
at the altar of some man. I'd also held fervent born-again
Christians in a little contempt, thinking them close-minded
and exclusionary at best and downright dangerous at worst.
Over time, I've noticed that my contempt, especially prior to
investigation, often stems from the root of my real problem,
which is fear. So, in my ongoing attempt to see and be free of
unnecessary fear, I decided to suspend my judgment and go
check out for myself what this born-again Christian business
was all about.

I took my charge seriously. I went to services almost every
Sunday for about a year, attended Christianity 101 class during the week, held prayer meetings in my home, and even got
christened again, just in case. In the end, I couldn't accept
some of the dogma and didn't buy that their way was the only
way, so we parted ways, but I no longer felt contemptuous. It
was like I had moved in with Jesus, found out that he was a really great guy, but failed to fall in love. Jesus was like many of
my ex-boyfriends. I still liked him a lot, and we were on very
good terms. But in the end, it just wasn't a match made
in heaven.

"You're doing what?" my friend Kaye asked when I told
her about my plans to socialize with convicted felons in a
maximum-security prison. "Wendy, isn't Internet dating dangerous enough?!" she said, alarmed. "*Please* don't give any of
these guys your phone number," she pleaded, "and whatever

you do, don't pick up any pen pals," her obvious concern based on my track record of being attracted to unavailable men combined with my willingness to go to any lengths to get what I thought I wanted.

"Re-lax," I assured her. "These men are in *prison,* and I'm just going to play *tennis,*" I repeated slowly, as if she hadn't fully understood me the first time around.

Kaye sighed. "Wendy," she said, "do you even play tennis?"

"I hardly think that matters. I look fabulous holding a racket," I said. "Besides, I'm just going for the experience," I told her, making a mental note to ask Alex how he planned to explain my tennis ineptitude to the team.

It took a while to decide on my outfit. Prison play-date visitors weren't allowed to wear any shade of blue, or blue jeans, or white or orange or yellow because those are the colors that the inmates wear, and they want visitors to stand out. Alex thought that I should also rule out pink and red, because they were too similar to orange (although I also suspect that to him, pink and red were just too sinful). So this left black, beige, brown, and green. No sexy clothing. No skirts or dresses or shorts. I wonder what a sporty nun might wear? As I dug through my closet, I realized that my options were limited.

In my ongoing effort to get out of my funk, I had recently tried adjusting my attitude with an "out with the old, in with the new" approach. I figured that until I was willing to let go of ideas and attitudes that no longer fit, I would never have room for anything new. So I decided to start by cleaning out my closet.

Out went my "fat" clothes, the large, baggy, schleppy items left over from my bulimia days, when the feel of a waistband lightly brushing against my stomach could send me into a panic. Out went the skintight off-the-shoulder black minidress that rode up my ass and the matching high heels that were impossible to walk in. Both extremes of this spectrum represent my intense and opposing desire to be both hidden and seen, and anything that whispered, "Don't look at me, I'm hideous," or screamed, **"I NEED ATTENTION!"** was thrown onto the pile.

These clothes were like uniforms for the Low Self-Esteem Club (LSEC), something like a Junior League for the self-loathing. I'm not sure when I had joined their ranks, but I felt like I'd been a dues-paying, card-carrying member for too long. I'd agreed with Groucho Marx when he said, "I'd never join a club that would have me as a member," but it seemed hard to resign, like trying to leave the Mafia. Did I need to fake my own death in order to escape my old ideas about myself and really enjoy my life? I hoped this Goodwill run would signify my official resignation and mark the beginning of a new era.

When I was younger and still drinking, the clothes in my closet evidenced my split personality. By day, I had a corporate job and wore conservative business suits with Dianne Feinstein–like blouses (you know the ones, with the big floppy bows that tie at the collar) and oversized red Annie Hall–ish glasses, and by night I roamed around San Francisco's Tenderloin district looking for trouble with my gay assistant from work (my then-boyfriend), occasionally being mistaken for a hooker in my black leather miniskirt and ripped fishnets. (I *know,* but it was the eighties. . . . Think Madonna in *Desperately Seeking Susan.*) I used to call these Jekyll-and-Hyde outfits "dressing defensively," as though clothes and makeup would shield me from the world. And they did, but because I was defining myself by whatever outfit I was wearing, I was constantly confused about who I was.

As I continued to inventory my remaining wardrobe for appropriate prison attire, I came across my oldest pair of blue jeans. You know the ones, the favorite ripped comfortable pair that are so worn out they are indecent, but for some reason you just can't quite part with them and still try to wear them every once in a while? I used to live in these things, I thought as I rubbed the thinning fabric against my cheek. I briefly considered getting rid of them, wondering what life would be like without them, before reflexively tossing them back into the closet.

As I dug deeper, I realized that I no longer even had any black pants. Weird. I remembered a time when the only color I wore was black. Now I had lots of blue, white, and—what's this?—even pink pants with a big bow on them! Yikes! Who was this new me?

What would Jesus wear? I wondered, rummaging through

my bureau, finally finding baggy brown linen clamdiggers and a beige T-shirt buried in a forgotten drawer.

Next I opened my lingerie drawer and weighed my options. I sure didn't want to visit San Quentin and win any accidental booby prizes. Do I go with a thickly padded bra that makes my boobs look bigger but would conceal any nipple action, or a lightly padded bra that won't call as much attention to that area and, barring any sudden cold drafts, should keep my nipples in solitary confinement? Or should I choose a sports bra that would offer good support while mashing and binding? Sheer lingerie is definitely out, and I think I can leave the water bra in the drawer. It might rupture during a security pat-down and start a flash flood.

Men always talk about big breasts, but in my experience what they are really focused on is the nipple. They get that glazed, dreamy look when getting a really good nipple shot through clothing, as though witnessing a female erection or returning to the time when the nipple was the primary focus of their life, shortly before they switched allegiance to their penises. Maybe men who aren't nipple-centric and prefer women in thick push-up bras are the ones who were bottle-fed instead of breast-fed, so they never developed a taste for the real thing. I'll have to ask.

Don't overthink this, Wendy, I thought. You are a B cup at best and in no danger of being mistaken for Pamela Anderson, so just go with a maximum-security padded bra and get ready!

I pulled on my clothes and looked in the mirror. This is

about as dressed down as I can get, I thought as I threw an imaginary tennis ball up for a practice swing and, freezing in an arms-over-the-head position, checked out the result. Definitely can't see my figure. No makeup. Hair in a ponytail. Sunglasses. Okay, good to go.

San Quentin is perched on the edge of San Francisco Bay, with a billion-dollar view of the city. I parked in the lot, which sits below the prison, and sat down by the water, watching the sailboats and seagulls. I could smell the pungent ocean air and felt for a moment that everything was just as it should be, something that I hadn't experienced for a while, and I was grateful for the reprieve from the constant volleying inside my head. I had been at odds with myself for months after another disappointing love affair left me confused and hurt—a state with which I had become all too familiar. My mind bounced back and forth between blaming him and punishing myself, and not unlike the weary, worn fabric of my beloved jeans, this perpetual feeling of unhappiness was wearing very thin. I had tried Internet-dating my blues away, but it felt like I was shopping at the hardware store for a book of poetry, and I was discouraged. I guess I'm feeling a little sorry for myself, I thought, like there are forces at work conspiring against me. I sighed, knowing perfectly well that those forces were in me. Maybe I'm supposed to learn something while I'm captive to this frame of mind, I thought, and got up to go to jail.

As I ran up the drive that led to the entrance, a guard started yelling at me and waving his arms. I slowed down, and when I got to the front door, he said, "Are you *trying* to get shot?" Apparently, running in and around prison is a no-no, and they had armed guards on the roof trained to be on alert for "runners."

"Sorry," I said sheepishly, recognizing that I was entering a zone of authority other than my own.

I saw Alex, and he introduced me to the other members of the Tennis God Squad. "Wendy is here to observe and help us scout for future tennis players," he explained, addressing my inability to actually play the game.

As part of the entry process, we were required to go through multiple checkpoints, and as we passed through each new level of security, the air pressure seemed to change, as though we were going back in time. Built in the 1850s, the prison looked like a medieval fortress, so much so that electricity seemed out of place. I suddenly imagined a guard in full armor on horseback chasing an escaped convict running barefoot in rags past the prison gates toward freedom. I found myself rooting for her to escape. Wait. It was a "her," and she looked startlingly familiar. Wait, it was me, and I was making a run for it. I snapped out of my Middle Ages fantasy to the sound of clanging steel doors behind me. Who was she really running from? I wondered absently as we emerged into the exercise yard at the heart of the prison.

I don't know if it was testosterone or oppression or fear or what, but the tension was palpable and I felt a little bit like

Dante. This place is a hard-core prison, I thought. What the hell have I gotten myself into?

At the same time, it was a gorgeous, clear day, and the prison yard had spectacular views of majestic Mount Tamalpais. The contrast between the beautiful Marin County exterior and the harsh interior atmosphere was startling yet familiar. The exercise yard was at the heart of the prison and was teeming with about three hundred men in prison garb, some working out on punching bags and weights, others milling around in little groups. The "privileged" inmates were all wearing light blue hats that matched their blue outfits and were warming up on the nearby basketball and tennis courts, and the sound of dribbling basketballs and of fists hitting heavy body bags echoed around the yard.

This looks like recess in, well, prison, I thought.

We were met by our host, Virgil, a beefy African-American inmate who looked about forty years old, had a tooth missing in the front, and a big angel tattooed on his right forearm. As he smiled and stuck out his angelic hand for introductions, I felt nervous, like I was cautiously approaching a pit bull that had suddenly wagged his tail.

"We tried to get some chairs with cushions because they told us that there was a woman coming, but we couldn't find any," he said apologetically, gesturing toward the hard white plastic chairs lined up along the tennis court. "We all came from women, and women should be respected," he continued, pulling up a chair for me.

I wasn't used to being characterized as a mother and nervously attempted a joke, saying that women had more padding in that area anyway. But as I looked into his eyes, I realized he was trying to show me respect and that my offhanded remark just wasn't going to cut it.

"Thank you for being so thoughtful," I said, shyly accepting his gesture and his show of respect and sitting down.

"You won't be hassled here," he assured me, smiling broadly, and I felt that by acknowledging his thoughtfulness, I had given him a gift.

"So why are you here?" I asked him as the first tennis game got under way. I felt uncomfortable, like I had committed to a blind dinner date in a bad neighborhood and was already looking forward to getting the check.

He explained that nineteen years ago he had been a crack addict involved in robbing a drugstore, that the clerk had been shot and killed by Virgil's "crime partner," and Virgil himself had been subsequently sentenced to prison for aiding and abetting. He had been clean and sober for eighteen of the nineteen years of his incarceration and was looking forward to July for his release date to be scheduled.

I started to relax a little. I had been clean and sober in AA for many years and knew how to talk to sober alcoholics.

"How many of the guys in here do you think have drug and alcohol problems?" I asked.

"Oh man, I'd say seventy to eighty percent at least," he said. "We have meetings five days a week, NA [Narcotics Anonymous] and AA. Mostly we try to shore up the guys who are going back out into the world. You know, they trade in their prison blues for street clothes, get on a bus to go home, and they get dropped off right in front of a liquor store. What are they gonna do then? I see them coming on back in here time and time again, doing life in prison on the installment plan because they aren't willing to do it differently."

"Prison blues?" I asked. "Is that what you call the blue outfits or their state of mind?"

"Both," he said.

Suddenly, Virgil, who had been standing next to my chair, crouched down and froze, as though dodging a bullet. I looked around and everyone else in the yard was also crouched down or frozen in position. This is surreal, I thought, like an episode of *The Twilight Zone* when the whole world stops, except for me. I felt like everyone else was in on the game and I was the only one who didn't know the rules. Shouldn't I have been given some sort of orientation booklet or something?

"Is everyone taking a little time out?" I whispered to Virgil, now crouched beside me.

He looked up at me with something like amusement and said, "No, Wendy, it's a lockdown. An alarm sounds when someone is being attacked or there is an incident in the yard. Everyone not involved in the fight has to crouch and freeze so that the guards can more easily contain the situation. It will be over in a minute, so sit tight."

Wow, I thought, I didn't even hear the alarm. Maybe that's

part of my problem. Alarms sound, whistles are blown, red flags are raised, signs are posted, and I just don't hear them, can't see them. Maybe I could try to use the apparent lockdown of my current mind-set to help sort out my confusion. Introduce an alarm and mandate that everything *real* in my head freezes so that everything left thrashing around can be seen for what it is: FEAR—False Evidence Appearing Real. But first I need to learn how to listen, I thought as I heard the bell sound, indicating that we were free to resume our activity.

Virgil convinced me to take a turn on the court. As I said, I don't really play tennis, but what the hell, I thought, I'm game to try. I stood at the edge of the penalty line and bounced the ball. The one thing I could do was serve, I just wasn't very good at volleying. I threw the ball up in the air and executed a perfect serve. It would be the only time that my racket actually connected with anything other than air. "Keep your eye on the ball," Virgil yelled as I continued to swing and miss with gusto, feeling a little foolish. This made for a very short game, but at least if I had to lose, I liked that my score was always love, and the other prisoners seemed to appreciate my willingness to try. I felt a little like the prison team mascot.

Afterward, Virgil and I took a walk around the yard among the general population. I felt uneasy again and unsure how to behave. Some of these guys are in here for life, I thought, and some of them could be in line behind me at Starbucks next week. Not sure who was more frightening to me, I nervously scanned the crowd to see if I recognized any of the faces from match.com. Settle down, I thought, this is not a speed-dating event.

At first I tried to heed Kaye's advice not to draw attention to myself and averted my gaze as we walked by groups of inmates milling around the yard. But after a while, I mustered up my courage and started looking into their faces and smiling. Sometimes they would smile back and say, "Hi, how're ya doing," but even when they didn't say anything, I was acknowledged with a nod or a friendly gesture. They seemed genuinely happy to see me, and I didn't feel objectified, even though in many cases I'm sure I was. Maybe it was the padded bra, or because I was not dressed to attract attention, or simply because once any possibility of sex or a real relationship is off the table, I'm more available for what's really there. Then again, it could have been the seven armed guards watching me at all times for signs of trouble. Still, I felt respected. More respected than I often did by more "respectable" men in the world at large. Oddly, I felt safe. I wonder who's different in here, I thought, me or men? (Alex later told me if anyone *had* disrespected me, our prison hosts would have kicked their asses, but it seems to me that having a good reason to act respectful, even if the reason was not wanting to get your ass kicked, was a start.)

As I really looked into each man's face, I started to see glimpses of something with which I was all too familiar: low self-esteem. It was a flicker in their eyes, like a secret handshake known only by alumni of the school of the insecure. I guess they had good reason to feel insecure; they were in prison. What's my excuse?

Dostoevsky wrote that the best way to keep a prisoner from escaping is to make sure that he doesn't know that he's in prison. It seemed clear from Virgil's story that changing outfits and being released from jail wasn't always enough to set these inmates free. I wondered what beliefs these men were holding on to that kept them in chains, in and out of prison. There's prison, like the one that I was standing in, and then there's prison, like the one that I was living in. How long had I been locked up? And what stories had I been etching on the prison cell walls of my mind? That I wasn't lovable? That I wasn't deserving of true happiness? I felt like I had been in solitary confinement for too long and wondered what it would take to be freed. Maybe instead of spending my time looking for a date, I should work on scheduling my release date, I thought. As Sartre says, "Freedom is what you do with what's been done to you."

We made our way over to watch the basketball game in progress on the other side of the yard. Prison B-ball was a little more confusing than usual because there were so many coaches. There was the outside team coach, the regular inside coach for the prison team, and then all the gang coaches for each gang member on the team, all of them shouting at once. This looks like the madness in my head, I thought, but somehow here, the chaos worked.

"Who's that?" I asked, pointing to one of the players, who

seemed to float across the court and looked like the happiest guy alive.

"That's Rob," Virgil said. "He's in here for life, with no chance of parole."

"Why does he look so happy?" I asked.

"He's committed himself to being of service and coordinates this whole program from the inside. He's been *saved*."

I nodded slowly as I watched Rob high-five someone from the opposing team. I guess there are different ways to be born again, I thought, and remembered that according to Jesus, man's greatest need was to be forgiven. If Rob had found freedom while locked in a maximum-security prison for life, then I guess it really was an inside job. Or, as the O'Neal Twins sing, "Jesus dropped the charges."

As I continued to watch the game unfold, a completely different picture started to emerge, like watching a Polaroid develop. I began to see that right now, at this moment, these weren't "good" guys from the outside playing "bad" guys from the inside at all. These were all just guys, on the court, playing ball, and as long as they were in the game, the playing field was level, and they were free. I noticed the men in the game looked a lot happier than the general population milling around the yard, killing time until recess was over.

As if reading my mind, one of the scarier-looking gang coaches yelled to a player from the sidelines, "We a team right now, and after the game's over we go back to jail, so play the game!" Maybe we are all just doing time in our own way, I thought, and the winners in life are the ones who know that it's a privilege to be allowed to stay in the game. I guess it's just up to me to decide how I want to play it.

As we were preparing to leave, Virgil presented me with a dark blue baseball hat with "San Quentin State Prison Tennis Coach" embroidered across the front. "Stay sweet," he said, and as he shook my hand good-bye, I could swear I saw the angel on his arm smiling.

I put my hat on and turned to take one last look around the yard at the other inmates in their prison blues and matching hats. Once the game was over, their hats would probably end up a status symbol at best, or a commodity at worst, and mine may eventually end up in the back of my closet or in the Goodwill pile. But for this moment, on this bright, beautiful day inside of San Quentin State Prison, it felt like we were all playing for the same team.

LONG-DISTANCE BILL

i **looked at** the flyer again as I was packing for the SLAA (Sex and Love Addicts Anonymous) retreat that ironically was being held at a monastery in Malibu, California.

"Billy, it says here that this retreat is for *identified* sex and love addicts only. That means when I introduce myself I have to say, 'Hi, I'm Wendy, and I'm a sex and love addict!' "

I had agreed to go on this weekend with Billy as sort of a last resort (and not the tropical vacation kind) in our on-again, off-again long-distance (him: Los Angeles; me: Sausalito) relationship, but I wasn't prepared to identify myself as a sex and love addict and join yet another twelve-step program for which I probably qualified.

"So what's the big deal?" Billy said. "It's all the same thing.

Love addiction, alcoholism, co-dependency—you got it all, baby!" He continued, "John Bradshaw was an alcoholic and co-dependent and a sex and love addict and didn't get into SLAA recovery until he was like seventeen years sober," referring to the fact that I had been sober in AA for almost as many years. Billy idolized John Bradshaw, an ex-monk turned therapist who was a primary figure in the self-help movement. Billy had a Bradshaw-ism for every occasion.

"No," I said, "it's you who has it all, Mr. I'm in Ten Different Twelve-Step Programs, Master of None." On our first date, he'd revealed that he had attended numerous twelve-step meetings, including SLAA, AA, Al-Anon (for co-dependents involved with addicts), BDA (Business Debtors Anonymous), CoDA (Co-dependents Anonymous), ACA (Adult Children of Alcoholics), NA (Narcotics Anonymous), MA (Marijuana Anonymous), DA (Debtors Anonymous), and EA (Emotions Anonymous).

How very L.A. (Los Angeles).

At the time, I found this intriguing and, my curiosity having got the better of me, agreed to a second date. Usually on a first date, if I share that I am a divorced, sober alcoholic over forty with abandonment issues, this is enough information to scare the guy away. Apparently, this strategy doesn't have the same effect on other addicts, and Billy far outweighed me in the TMI (too much information) department.

"Yep, that's me, all right," he said proudly as he picked me up and swung me around, both of us falling onto his king-size bed.

"So, will we have to break up this weekend because when we look directly at our addictive behavior we will realize that we shouldn't be together?" I said nervously, untangling myself from his arms and rolling onto my side to look at him as we lay side by side on his bed. God, why did he have to feel so good, I thought. *Like whiskey,* my mind replied.

"No," he said, squirming. "Do you want to break up with me?"

"No," I said. Yes, I thought. This was our fourth go-round, and the last time we got back together we had targeted this weekend as the wait-and-see point. Billy was "working" on his sex- and love-addiction issues and thought that if I went to this retreat with him and became more familiar with his disease, I might gain some insight into our relationship. (I believe this type of thinking qualifies us both for CoDA.)

Billy had been a blind date arranged through his beautiful ex-girlfriend Nicola, whom I had met through my friend Paul. "I think you two would like each other, and he wants a girlfriend," she said when she brought up the idea of setting us up. I liked *her* a lot, and it seemed like getting a boyfriend referral from a beautiful woman whom I respected was as good a reason as any to check him out.

"I'm totally willing to put all other women aside to get to know you," he said as I bit into my burrito at the taco stand to which he had taken me on our first date. (He wasn't eating; he was on the Master Cleanse, which means drinking nothing but a mixture of lemon, maple syrup, cayenne pepper, and water for a week. It's an L.A. thing). Somehow he had known exactly what I needed to hear in order to get me into the game, and I took the bait. Of course, that was before we had sex. A month later, he was singing the "We don't want to rush into anything serious" blues, which translates in man language to: "I want to be free to see other people." I didn't like this concept, but not wanting to completely upset the applecart, I didn't push it, and instead I tried to take it "one date at a time."

Shortly after that, I stumbled across (and by "stumbled," I mean I went to a great deal of trouble to find it) one of his many online profiles, in which he described himself as completely available and actively seeking his "soul mate." I noticed that he had posted a recent picture of himself that I had taken. My heart sank.

When I called him on it, he took his profile offline for two days, then broke up with me via e-mail, saying, "There are four things I'll never do: gay sex, child molestation, heroin, or long-distance relationships. And besides," he stated, "we aren't boyfriend/girlfriend, and this isn't a serious relationship, so we aren't even breaking up." Somehow the long-distance thing hadn't been a problem for him until he needed it to be.

Furious, I replied via e-mail, "Not serious? What do you call taking me to your therapy sessions, leaving notes around the house that said, 'I could love Wendy,' telling me that I met all your 'dream-woman' criteria, and reiterating how compatible we were, how great the sex was, how we complemented each other, how much you needed my touch, how you wanted a partner, and how you had put all other women aside to get to know me? That constitutes 'not serious' to you?!" I signed off with an angry, fist-shaking smiley face from my online smiley face collection.

"Well, maybe moderately serious," he amended. "But just remember, rejection is God's protection!"

"Fuck you!" I typed back, wishing I had a smiley face that could flip him the bird.

"Bradshaw says to use your 'I' language to express how you feel when you are angry," he shot back.

"Okay, *I* think that you're an asshole," I finished, unable to identify an adequate smiley face to express feeling hurt and betrayed.

That was Round 1.

Round 2 began when I asked him to come to Sausalito and spend Christmas with me. I know, there's a disconnect here, right? You did what? How could you think it was going to be different? you ask. I didn't, but I was lonely and could only see as far as getting through the holidays. This was my short-term gain/long-term pain thinking in action. I tried to rationalize (or "rationale *lies*," as I like to call it) that I would have more control over my emotions now that I knew he was a jerk. I also now felt superior to him, so I believed that my self-righteousness would keep me in a position of power. I mean, I wouldn't actually get *attached* to a jerk once I knew better, right? If I could have been totally honest with myself, I would have seen that I was really just in pain and looking for a quick fix. They say that addicts will pay any price tomorrow to get their needs met today. "They" are right.

"I'll be your Mr. December," he joked, and I agreed, as though the month of December was the mating season to be jolly, and come January I could just move on, unfazed.

I could not, and in January I fell back into my pattern of spending a week in L.A. and a week at home. Dating Mr. December in January was like leaving a Christmas tree in the living room way past the holiday season, and jolly turned into folly. The tree, like us, was only meant to be seasonal and soon sagged under the weight of my new year "sexpectations." Billy confessed that he had started going out with several other women, and he felt guilty about it. Felt that I was *like* his girl-friend but not really. (Sadly, we weren't even a real tree.) Indignantly, as though he had somehow done me wrong yet again, I flounced home. If I couldn't have it my way, I didn't want to play. After my self-righteousness died down, I felt abandoned and rejected, and spent the next several months licking my wounds.

Fast-forward to June. I'm feeling better and getting on with my life but still secretly obsessing about him. Every once in a while he would send me an e-mail, testing my resolve, to see if I wanted a "boyfriend" for the weekend. I did, and I didn't. My heart was starting to heal, yet I missed him, or maybe I just missed the feeling I had when I was with him—that feeling of being sexually desirable, if nothing else. (Was there a smiley face for this?) I knew from the day that we got back together the first time that he wasn't the right guy for me, that I couldn't really count on him, yet I got attached. Just call me Velcro Girl. But I also knew that I wasn't ready to leave well enough alone. I didn't like the way we had left it, didn't even know how to characterize our trysts. What do you call someone you dated who never made it to boyfriend status? A booty call? It was more than that. An ex-lover? That sounds too romantic for this guy. Some guy I dated? Not substantial enough for the emotional repercussions involved. No, at the very least I wanted ex-girlfriend status with Billy. After some fairly complicated negotiations, Billy agreed to a trial monogamous "boyfriend/girlfriend" arrangement for an open-ended period of time with an opt-out clause. Maybe all this was just romantic semantics, but thinking that I could somehow put the "fun" back into dysfunctional, I went in for Round 3.

Round 3 ended several months later, on his birthday, when he broke up with me yet again, only to call me back three days later to say that he had changed his mind, made a terrible mistake, and wanted one more chance, targeting this retreat weekend as our make-or-break date. Enter Round 4.

i thought about all of this as I lay on his bed, looking into his beautiful face. He was a sexy combination of John Cusack and Kevin Spacey and had the longest eye-lashes I had ever seen on a man. And he knew it. I sighed. We looked so beautiful together in the world, his six-feet-four tall, dark, and handsome coupled with my six-feet-one long, lean, and blond. Of course, my friends thought, Why is Wendy wasting her time with this guy? They could see what I could not: the neon sign just above those long lashes that flashed, TOXIC MANHOLE—BEWARE ALL YE WHO ENTER! I've always been attracted to neon but was clearly partially blinded by it; all I could read was ENTER!

There are signs, and then there are signs. A few weeks ago, we had been driving on Highway 101 in Marin County, where billboards aren't allowed, and I commented, "Isn't it peaceful and nice driving down the highway without all those signs?" He heard me but didn't say anything. Until much later, when we were driving down Sunset Boulevard in Hollywood, where billboards are as ubiquitous as breast implants, and he suddenly said, "I like billboards; they're pretty. Look at that giant one of a girl's perfect ass over there. I don't know what they're selling and I don't care!"

I knew that he meant this from the bottom of his heart. Billy had lived in Hollywood for fifteen years. He had adapted to his environment. I realized that Billy had become a Billy-board, a larger-than-life advertisement for a real person that always, always promised more than it could deliver. Why oh why do I keep buying this stuff? Sadly I knew what he was selling, knew

I was paying above market value, and didn't care. I must be adapting, too.

Maybe I was a love addict after all. I certainly had all the information I needed about this man to know that he wasn't a good bet for a real relationship. Why couldn't I make a clean break? How many times did I have to watch this rerun? There were plenty of other warning signs. The fact that he was a broke, insecure actor who craved constant attention and flirted outrageously, had pictures of beautiful, sexy women plastered all over his bedroom, kept *Playboy* magazines in the bathroom, rarely actually attended any twelve-step meetings, let alone worked a program of recovery, was forty-two and had never been in a successful relationship, had sex with his female therapist before briefly sponsoring her in SLAA (a sponsor is an objective, recovered person who has worked the twelve steps and can lead a newcomer through the program of recovery— Billy did not qualify), and was still "friends" with Nicola, who, although she didn't want him for keeps, still wanted his sperm for artificial insemination. And last but not least, his opening remark as we sat in his therapist's office shortly after embarking on Round 3.

"Wendy is the only girlfriend I've ever had that I wasn't in love with," he said, "and I refuse to fall in love with anyone who lives out of town." This alone should have been enough. Really. Enough for me to pick up my purse, fling my long blond hair over my shoulder, and sweep out, saying something pithy like "And you are the only boyfriend I've needed to fake an or-gasm with" (certainly not true) or something mature like "You know, I'm not actually in love with you either, so let's call it a day, shall we?" then shake hands and part as friends.

But denial is a funny thing. Instead of focusing on the "I'm not in love with you" part, I focused on the "You don't live here" part and proceeded to pretend to move to L.A. True, I spend a lot of time there and had been considering relocating, but now I was on a mission. I work in advertising. I know how to put together a campaign. Having achieved temporary "girl-friend" status, I decided that the objective of this new campaign was to get Billy to fall in love with me. My strategies were to appear to be serious about moving and, in the process, con-vince him that he couldn't live without me. I wasn't really sure what would happen after that.

My friend Paul was. "You don't want this guy, Wendy. You just want him to want you, and as soon as he does, you'll dump him because you will finally be able to see that he's a jerk," he said wearily over lunch in Beverly Hills. "You are casting pearls before swine," he finished as I took a big bite of my BBQ pork sandwich.

I could hear Paul talking, but his words didn't make it past my internal security checkpoint. His point was confiscated and thrown onto the pile where anything sharp enough to puncture my ego often ended up, like a heap of nail clippers, scissors, and penknives at airport security.

"I've always wanted to live in L.A.," I had told Billy as I

signed up with online rental agencies, looked feverishly for apartments. I finally ended up subletting a friend's furnished apartment to prove to myself and him that I was serious about moving. I could run my business from anywhere and proceeded to do just that.

And now here we are, I thought, pulling myself up off the bed to finish packing for the weekend finale.

the retreat facility was a noble

old monastery high atop a mountain in Malibu overlooking the Pacific Ocean. Billy and I were sharing a bedroom but had separate beds, à la *The Dick Van Dyke Show,* and were encouraged to abstain from sex for the weekend. Billy unpacked while I walked around the romantic monastic gardens with a killer view of the beaches far below. Will this overlook come to represent make-out point or breakup cliff? I wondered absently.

I felt nervous about being there, like an imposter. I knew how to attract sex and love addicts; I just didn't know if I was one, or even what that meant. I had dated a whole spectrum of addicts, both in and out of recovery, and tended to think I knew what their problems were and how to solve them: that if only they would take my advice, everything would be fine. This more than qualifies me for Al-Anon and CoDA, but I've heard it said that if you can spot it, you got it, and that made me nervous. *Hmm,* let's see, what else have I spotted? The twelve-step men I've dated include alcoholics (usually intelligent, self-

centered, charismatic, handsome man/boys with mother issues), a few recovering hardcore drug addicts (often charming
mentally ill liars; recovering heroin addicts are the worst—they
will steal your wallet and then help you look for it), one hor-
rendous gambling addict (always betting on the come), co-
dependents (needy, controlling, and insecure: addicted to the
addict), and now a sex and love addict (who uses sex to manage his feelings and is terrified of emotional intimacy). If these
men were all mirrors, what did that say about me? I knew it was
time to stop focusing on their behavior and start looking at
mine. But looking directly at *my* behavior usually resulted in
change, and change, even for the better, always scared me. This
weekend scared me.

The retreat began, and we were divided into separate
groups, men in one room, women in the other. The women's
room was a wood-paneled, sparsely furnished chamber with a
fireplace and floor-to-ceiling windows. How very *Thorn Birds*,
I thought. We sat in chairs arranged in a circle and all took turns
introducing ourselves. "Hi, I'm Zandra, and I'm a love addict."
"Hi, Zandra!" everyone replied. "Hi, my name is Francis and
I'm a compulsive masturbator." "Hi, Francis!" "Hello, my name
is Edith, and I'm a sexual anorexic." "Hi, Edith!" As the introductions worked their way around the circle toward me, I
started to panic. These descriptions sounded very complicated,
and I had no idea what to call myself in SLAA, so when it was
my turn, I said, "Hi, I'm Wendy, and I'm not sure what I am, except here." This seemed to satisfy everyone, and they nodded

knowingly and said, "Hi, Wendy!" as though it was only a matter of time. I was afraid they were right. Later, during the sharing portion of the meeting, I said, "I don't really understand sex and love addiction; it's different from substance abuse. In AA, either you are drinking or you are not. How do you define sobriety here?"

In between sessions, love addict Zandra, a successful Hollywood screenwriter and Jennifer Garner lookalike (why do so many people in L.A. look like movie stars?), pulled me aside and explained that everyone was different and there were many degrees of addiction. That each person defines her own "bottom-line" self-destructive behaviors, and her willingness to act out those behaviors or not determined her "sobriety."

"Can you give me some examples?" I said, rubbing my temples.

"Some people are promiscuous, and abstaining from compulsive sex with strangers defines success. Others are addicted to fantasy and porn. And some, like me, are love addicts, who fall in love with unavailable people and end up obsessed and miserable," she said. (*Ding ding ding!*)

As she was talking, my mind became a bad game-show network, and I suddenly landed in *Jeopardy!* "*Alex, I'd like 'Love Addicts' for a thousand please,*" I say. "*You got it, Wendy!*" Alex responds. "*Here's your answer, and good luck! 'A popular woman writer who keeps falling into manholes.' *" I draw a blank. I can't think. I know I should know this one! I start feeling very anxious about getting the question to the answer right, and then concerned that I won't win the $1,000, and then worried that this concern qualifies me for GA (Gamblers Anonymous), and I feel tension mounting, and I dread the buzzer. I just need to get a clue, I think frantically, and suddenly Robert Palmer is singing, and I am backed, here on the *Jeopardy!* stage, by three stone-cold beauties from the "Addicted to Love" video. I am having an eighties flashback. I absently touch my hair to see how big it is. All at once, I remember that the question to the answer is me, and I call out, *"Who is Wendy Merrill?"* seconds before the yes bell dings, the *Jeopardy!* theme music cues up, and I flip back to our regularly scheduled programming.

Zandra was now telling me all about another program, LAA (Love Addicts Anonymous). Turns out there are many different kinds of LAs (Love Addicts, not to be confused with Los Angeles, or wait, maybe they're synonymous). There are OLAs (Obsessed Love Addicts), CLAs (Co-dependent Love Addicts), RAs (Relationship Addicts), NLAs, (Narcissistic Love Addicts), and ALAs (Ambivalent Love Addicts). She went on to describe each type, and I watched her mouth moving, reading her lips as though she had been muted, until she got to ALAs, and suddenly the audio was back.

"ALAs crave love but fear intimacy, so basically, they are screwed," she said. I wonder if she knows how funny that is, I think. "And there are many different kinds of ALAs," she said. Of course there are. She continued, using her fingers to enumerate each type. "There are the Torch Bearers, who obsess about someone who is unavailable and suffer some degree of unrequited love; the Saboteurs, who destroy relationships whenever they get serious enough for their fear of intimacy to come up; the Seductive Withholders, who run hot and cold, unless they actually leave the relationship—then they are Saboteurs—and the Romance addicts, who use sexual passion and pseudoemotional intimacy to bond shallowly with multiple partners—not to be confused with sex addicts, who don't bond at all."

Okay, I thought, so bottom line, if you eat your heart out over some unavailable person or another year after year, or sabotage one relationship after the next, have serial romantic affairs, or only feel close when you are with another avoidant, you may be an ALA.

FA (Fucking A)!

At this point, the break was over, and we filed back into the meeting room, but I had heard enough. The rest of the weekend was more of the same and continued to be illuminating, to say the least. By the time the retreat was almost over, I knew in my heart that Billy and I were, too. I knew what I had known all along: that he was never going to be available to me in the way that I wanted him to be—was never going to *love* me—and when I was really honest with myself, I didn't even know if I *liked* him. I may have been casting pearls before swine, but the pearls were fake.

I still didn't know what the answer to my never-ending pattern of picking these men was, but I was tired of the suffering and the pretending that this situation was ever going to change. I guess at least that was a start. Once I start to become aware of my behavior and actually name it, well, the fun's usually over. Or maybe the fun's just beginning. I always get that part confused.

The last day of the retreat, I sat in the gardens in reflection. As I stared out over the blue Pacific, trying to formulate my thoughts, the game-show network came back on and now it was *Wheel of Fortune* time. Vanna White was there, wearing a lovely white floor-length off-the-shoulder sequined evening gown with a long slit up the side. She was standing in front of the writing on the wall, waiting for me to say the words out loud so that she could turn around the last letter and I could win my prize.

THE __ND

I knew what the answer was, but still I was afraid to buy that last vowel. I could see that my relationship with Billy would not, could not continue, yet I couldn't quite call it. Why was I so good at starting these things and so terrible at ending them? Was it just that I was afraid of the feelings that would follow? *Hmm,* I guess that makes me an LA with a dash of CLA, heavy on the torch-bearing saboteur ALA with a smidge of RA. This is more confusing than ordering a coffee at Starbucks in LA! It's time to get back to northern CA, I thought, and I got up to finish packing.

The weather was unseasonably warm, and Billy and I ended the weekend with a walk along the beach. Vanna was still there, encouraging me (she's such a nice girl), revealing the letters of twelve-step idioms one by one: "Suit up, show up; you might just grow up," and "You are as sick as your secrets," and "You can recover, if you have the capacity to be honest." I took a deep breath and tried to follow Vanna's lead.

I told Billy how frightening it was for me to leave relationships, how it sometimes triggered a domino effect of abandonment and loss that resonated far beyond any current situation, and how it often felt like death to me. I tried to use my "I" language. "I just want to know that I matter to you, that I'm special, and can't be easily replaced," I said shyly. "Even if what we need to do is break up once and for all," I finished, trying to lay the groundwork for either the resolution or dissolution of our relationship.

He held my hand and nodded as though he understood, but I noticed him checking out a nearby bikini-clad woman out of the corner of his eye. I suddenly felt vulnerable and exposed, an oyster without a shell. Vanna shivered and I mentally brought her a sweater and some hot cocoa.

Walking back toward the car, I noticed a couple of sandpipers flirting with the water's edge. They ran back and forth with the waves, looking for their chance to feed. One of them was a shallow feeder who just pecked at the sand, looking for easy prey, never fully committing its beak before moving on to the next feeding opportunity, while the other, apparently his mate, buried its long neck so deeply into the sand that it was almost swept away by the incoming waves.

"That's the female," I commented, pointing. "The one with her head in the sand."

several weeks later, the day before New Year's Eve:

"I don't want to start the New Year on a false note," Billy said when he called to break up with me. My stomach dropped, but I was relieved and didn't argue. He was doing what I hadn't been able to, and I knew it was the right thing, knew I needed to get my head above ground and move on. "I just don't want to lose you from my life. I want us to be friends," he said, and I agreed. Maybe we had found our happy ending, I thought hopefully as I hung up the phone.

Two days later, I was sitting in my living room staring at the wall. There is often a time delay associated with me feeling my feelings, so that if you ask me how I am feeling today, I'll usually be able to get back to you with an answer in a couple of weeks. This is probably why the rehab counselors showed us an emotional smiley face chart, so that we could identify our feelings and learn to *express* ourselves. (Maybe that's why I liked the online smileys so much.) The chart had a range of smiley faces, or not-so-smiley faces, and I squinted, trying to remember what my choices were. My therapist, Rita, was always encouraging me to identify how I really felt, because, as she put it, "Fine is not a feeling, Wendy." Let's see, I thought, I think I'm feeling a little sad, but kind of okay. Is okay a feeling?

As I was contemplating the nuances between feeling so-so and iffy, Billy called me from his car to relay a cute story about a mutual friend of ours. I thought, Okay, he's checking in, being thoughtful, maybe we actually can be friends, and I felt melancholy yet loving toward him. ("Good girl!" I heard Rita saying.)

Until he stopped midstory and abruptly said, "I have to go; I'm meeting someone." My stomach clenched. Shit. I can't get through one phone conversation with this guy without feeling bad (okay, more specifically, hurt and rejected)!

"Who are you meeting?" I asked, wishing I hadn't.

"No one you know," he said.

"You have a *date*?" I said, incredulously.

"N-no, it's just a coffee thing," he stammered nervously.

"With a girl?" I said, unable to stop myself, and made a mental note to pick up a new Al-Anon meeting schedule.

"Well . . . yes," he said.

"So *you* are calling *me* on your way to meet some girl for a coffee date two days after we break up?" I asked, hating myself for asking but hating him more. "Where did you find this girl?"

"Um, well, I met her on Craigslist," he said.

"So you are calling me on your way to meet some girl for coffee whom you met *online* two days after we break up? What's this girl's name?" I said, feeling myself starting to fall, fumbling for the parachute I had neglected to wear.

"It's kind of funny. . . ." he said. "Her name, I mean, it's Wendy, but listen . . . I really have to get out of the car; I'm here and she's waiting."

"So let me get this straight," I said. "You are calling me on your way to a coffee date with some girl named *Wendy* whom you met online two days after we break up when you know that my greatest fear during a breakup is that I don't matter and that I'm easily replaced?!" My hands shook with adrenaline and I was in complete awe of both his thoughtlessness and my ability to deceive myself.

"Is this what you call being a friend?" I finally said.

"Listen, I have to go. I'll call you later!" he said, and hung up.

I was left holding the phone, shaking and baffled and *pissed*! I didn't even know where to start. I couldn't decide if I wanted to laugh or cry. Smiley faces were exploding all around me. Was he that malicious or that clueless? *Did I get it yet!?* Vindictive Wendy took hold for a minute and wanted to hurt him back. I remembered a recent check that I'd written him for some voice-over work that he'd done for my company. I immediately went online to cancel the check. As I hit "Stop Payment," it occurred to me that I needed to apply this action to more than just his check—that it was high time I stopped paying this ridiculously expensive man tax. I felt like such a fool, like I'd kept buying swampland in Florida long after I knew it was worthless, simply to justify my original purchase.

Vengeance is greedy, and still not satisfied, I called his cell phone and left a message. "You are such a jerk!" I said. "How could you do this to *me*!" Then I hung up, only vaguely aware that I was really just talking to myself.

He called me back about twenty minutes later and said, "You'll be happy to know that it was nothing, just some freaky girl I'll never see again. . . ."

"That's too bad, Billy," I said, "because that freaky little coffee date just cost you my friendship!"

I yelled indignantly for the next twenty minutes while he insisted that his only mistake was that he wasn't able to lie fast enough. When I couldn't take it anymore, I just hung up. As they say in SLAA, if you can't detach with love, then just detach. (Or is that Al-Anon? *Whatever!*)

I could *finally* say it: "THE END."

Well, not really. In the end, I reversed the canceled check—I had enough bad karma to contend with, without incurring more. In the end, I realized that my self-righteousness was really just my well-worn fear of not being good enough and that it was not Billy's job to convince me of my worth. In the end, I realized that I needed to know that I mattered and was special and irreplaceable—to me (ugh). In the end, I just had to surrender because, as John Bradshaw says, "the battle that you will always lose is the battle you fight with yourself." And finally, in the end, I realized that the real long-distance relationship was the one I was having with myself and that what I needed to do now was find a way to move closer to home.

CLIFF NOTES

i'd like to be able to say that after Billy, I was able to buy a first-class ticket back to myself and live happily ever after above ground, but, alas, this was not to be the case. There was apparently some additional field-work required in the seemingly endless curriculum of the school of hard knocks (or hard heads, or hard . . . never mind) before I could honestly say that I had lived *and* learned. It was more like, live and continue to yearn. And just so you don't think that I'm a complete loser with no social memory (or in case you got bored in the earlier chapters and skipped ahead to the "good parts"), and at the risk of being redundant, before I get into this next tale, I want to remind you of a couple of things about me that might help explain the next series of events.

Keep in mind that I was a late bloomer. I was the tall, scrawny tomboy on the sidelines of the seventh-grade dance floor wearing a miniskirt and white patent-leather go-go boots (stuffed with rags to fill them out), awkwardly holding my J. C. Penney's plastic fringed purse to cover my knock-knees, pretending not to care that nobody was asking me to dance, and dying inside. While other girls were determining who they were more like, Ginger or Mary Ann, Betty or Veronica, I knew in my heart of hearts that I was destined to be Olive Oyl. I ached to be Veronica, I longed to be Ginger—sexy, cunning, and desirable—but knowing that I was none of those things, felt certain that Archie and the Professor could never be mine, and the best I could hope for was Popeye.

A few years later, I turned into the sweet-sixteen, never-been-kissed good girl yearning to be bad who didn't have breasts to speak of (I'm still waiting for those) and was convinced that I was the tallest girl in the world, already over six feet, or, as I used to say, five feet, twelve inches. I never had a date in high school, and my "awkward period" lasted well into my twenties as my body slowly caught up with itself. My ideas about myself have been even slower to change, and a part of me has been forever frozen in time as that shy, dateless, braless teenage girl obsessed with wanting a popular boy who could at least reach her waist to ask her to dance and kiss her good night without a stepstool.

In short, I felt like a giant dork.

So, when I first saw Cliff at a party while on vacation in Maui, he looked like the "captain of the football team" kind of boy I never got the chance to dance with, much less date, in high school. He was six-three, with graying blond hair and striking blue eyes, the kind of eyes that at first glance were dreamy Brad Pitt blue but later, upon closer inspection, were a more ominous blue, like the color of the Maui water right before it drops off into an area locally known as "Shark Pit," where even though the water is shallow, danger lurks. In his late forties, he still looked like the all-American good boy/bad boy star football player he had undoubtedly been, with a broad chest, sexy arms, and a very tight end. He looked as though he could spring into action at any second and score a touchdown. All he seemed to need was someone to pass him the ball. Handsome, drunk, and apparently still trying to score, he was inexplicably waving his flashlight at women while they were dancing, like a slightly deranged disco ball. (He'd walked to the party and brought a flashlight so he could find his way home in the dark.)

Maybe he just needs the right woman, I mused as the beam of his flashlight suddenly reflected off my shiny belt buckle, momentarily blinding us both.

Pointing his baby blues in the general vicinity of my waistline, or what I had begun to refer to as my *waste*line (I hadn't even wanted to date in the six months since breaking up with Billy and had started to fear that I might be missing my sexual peak), he walked toward me, stuffing his flashlight into his back pocket. "Hi, I'm Cliff," he said as he extended his hand for introductions.

Our conversation, or rather his opening series of questions, went as follows: what he said and what I did *not* hear.

"Where are you from?" he asked. (Mandatory opening in a vacation-destination situation—does not necessarily imply genuine interest.)

"Who's your friend?" he said, referring to my girlfriend Hedy, with whom I had come and who was seated nearby. (*Threesome, anyone?*)

"Are you 'with her' with her?" (*Are you lesbian/bisexual and/or is there a threesome possibility?*)

"How long are you going to be here?" And with this question he tweaked the lacy thong underwear peeking out of the top of my skirt. (*Do I have time to seduce you and make a clean getaway?*)

After ascertaining that I would be on the island for a few weeks, Cliff quickly filled me in on his life. Again, what he said was vastly different from what I heard. He had in fact been a professional football player until a woman had broken his heart. So he'd moved to Nice, France, to lick his wounds and write, and had been living there for the past twenty years, except when he was living in Maui at his parents' vacation home on the beach.

What little Wendy heard was: He's a stud with a heart; he's exotic and brave, sensitive and artistic; he comes from money. And he likes me, he really likes me!

While he was talking, I (big Wendy) had two simultaneous thoughts: (1) He was suffering from arrested development, and (2) I was going to be sexually involved with him. There was clearly no relationship potential here, and I had never been one for casual sex. What was it about this guy that was tempting me to break my man fast? Sure, he was cute, but he was acting like a buffoon (at this point he had whipped out his flashlight and resumed his bizarre light-show behavior). Good sense would dictate that I break a fast with emotional carrot juice or sexual miso soup instead of mainlining horny, hot Bosco, but good sense seemed like a relatively abstract theory at that moment.

I read somewhere that when an addict has a strong and immediate sexual attraction to someone, it's best to turn and run, but why is that? Was it just a case of wounded child meets wounded child? What's fair about a universe where so many of the things that I seem to crave (bad boys, triple mocha lattes, shots of tequila, frosting out of the can, shopping online, reading *Us* magazine) are bad for me? If I'm attracted to this man, then surely there must be something good about him. Or is being attracted to Nice Guy the closest I can come to being attracted to a nice guy?

Putting his arm around my waist, he started to do the bump against my hip in time to the music, and suddenly realizing that I "liked him liked him," I became seventh-grade self-conscious, panicked slightly, and said, "Will you excuse me?" and went and hid in the bathroom.

"Get a grip," I said to the woman staring back at me from the bathroom mirror as I pulled back my long blond hair, which, with the help of a very expensive hairdresser, didn't look too much different from when I was sixteen. You are not a teenager anymore, I thought. You are a grown woman. True, he doesn't appear to be boyfriend material, but you've never dated anyone like him before (*liar!*), and he's probably just acting silly because he's drunk. You may not be ready to be in a real relationship, but you've been too afraid even to date for a while (or as I'd been telling my friends, "I'm closed for repairs"), so maybe it's time that you got back on that dance floor. I dare you! Besides, being on vacation means doing things you don't normally do at home, right? You don't normally have flings, so maybe he can be Vacation Fling Guy. I wonder what that would be like? He's tall, he's cute, he's sexy, lives on the beach, and seems relatively harmless. I should be able to handle this (*sigh*).

I dabbed my lips, adjusted my padded bra, and checking out my butt in the mirror, said aloud, "And who are you hiding from anyway, him or you?"

As I walked back toward the party, my stomach seized up. Was this butterflies or nausea? Infatuation or a warning sign? That sensation in the pit of my stomach usually indicated either euphoric excitement or anxious dread, depending on whatever meaning I attached to it. Right now it was a brackish euphoric dread. A nauseous butterfly.

At least I'll probably lose some weight, I rationalized (I called the anxiety I experience whenever engaging with someone new my "dating diet"), and followed the lights back into the party, a moth to the flame.

I attempted awkward conversation with Cliff for another half an hour, wondering when he would ask for my number. He didn't. He said, "Come by the house anytime, and let's go snorkeling," then recited his address.

The party was being held at a trendy Maui boutique that had a live web cam, so after Hedy and I returned to our condo that evening, I went to my computer and typed in their URL to do a little cyberstalking. The party was still in full force. I didn't see Cliff dancing with any of the pretty girls, but wait, was that him in the corner, slow-dancing with a mannequin? Was this jock behavior or jerk behavior? I wondered, almost hearing the tiny voice in the back of my head shouting, "Run!" (*Okay, ladies, I know what you are thinking, but haven't you ever seen a red light on your car dashboard blink, and you think, Did I really see that or was it just a little short circuit? It's probably nothing; it will be okay!*)

So, misinterpreting my instinct to flee as fear of dating, I consulted Hedy, who had met Cliff at the party. "Do you think that's him?" I said, pointing to the grainy image. "He asked me to go snorkeling with him," I said as she leaned in toward the screen to make out the identity of the mannequin dance partner. "Yeah, that's him, all right. Very impressive." She looked up at me from the screen with something like pity and said, "Honey, isn't going 'snorkeling' with this guy kind of like going to a whorehouse for a kiss?"

Now, I love Hedy, but she watches entirely too much Dr. Phil. "Dr. Phil had a show on this very situation last week" was usually the first thing out of her mouth when giving me dating advice, delivered with a slight Southern drawl. She has been more or less married since she was about twelve, but that *never* stops her, and this particular advice sounded like a direct quote from last week's show.

So I scoffed and turned off my computer, but I wondered, If this was the type of guy that I'm currently attracted to, what does that say about me? I never got any attention from boys when I was a teenager, but that was lifetimes ago. Why was I so ridiculously flattered by this man's attention? Am I the one who's really suffering from arrested development? Clearly I must be in some sort of perimenopausal puberty. How long will this last? Is this an actual phenomenon, like the single woman's version of a midlife crisis, or just specific to me?

If adult adolescence is some kind of phase that I must pass through in order to graduate to the next level of maturity in the school of relationships, maybe it's better that I work through it now, while I'm still in my forties, so that I don't have to be doing this in thirty years at some senior living facility. I'll have to ask Hedy if Dr. Phil has covered this on any of his shows, I thought, and picturing myself in orthopedic high heels flirting with an eighty-year-old version of Cliff wearing his letter jacket and dragging an oxygen tank, I turned off the lights and went to sleep.

The next day I woke up with laryngitis. Trying not to read too much into the fact that I'd decided to sleep with a man I'd just met and had now essentially lost my voice, I drove by his house and threw my business card in the mailbox. He called later that day, and plans to go "snorkeling" were made.

"I'm going to have a fling," I announced when I called to check in with my friend Paul, my world-class commitment-phobic Hollywood producer Jewish-mother man friend whom you've already met.

"Wendy," he said, "you don't have flings, you have relationships. You are not a fling girl. And what's wrong with your voice? Is this one of those situations where I should throw my body in front of you and bar the door? Do I need to fly out there? Don't you remember what happened when you tried to have a fling with Billy? When are you coming home?"

"No, *no!*" I insisted, "This is different; it's a *vacation* fling. He lives in France, for God's sake! Don't worry! Listen," I continued, "I can't hear you very well. My cell reception is bad. I love you! I'll call you later!" (Note to self: Pretending to lose cell-phone reception with a well-meaning friend while rationalizing having a fling indicates descent into manhole. In future, please remember to proceed with caution or consider alternative route.)

The first time I had sex with Cliff, he shaved me. "Girls in France are always shaved," he said as he brought out the electric razor and slid a towel underneath me. "Okay," I said, struggling to be nonchalant and failing. This feels awkward, I thought, like I'm being prepped for surgery, but hey, you are Vacation Fling Girl, so just go with it.

The sex itself was okay. Right out of the playbook, and while he covered all of the bases, what Cliff couldn't do was kiss—and for me, it's all about the kiss. Afterward, feeling a little lonely, I was drifting off to sleep with my back to Cliff when he did something so awful, so terrible, that it should really be documented somewhere as being completely against fling rules. He reached around my shoulder and, finding my hand, which was tucked securely under my pillow, he held on to it tightly, for hours. I was hooked. I might just as well have been a lizard getting her belly rubbed instead of a woman who just got her pussy shaved. Big Wendy may think she wants sex, but little Wendy wants love.

Over the next ten days, Cliff played me romantic love songs from the forties, songs that made me sick with love, like "Bewitched, Bothered and Bewildered" and "I'm in the Mood for Love." He took me snorkeling, kayaking, and water-skiing, and each night we would watch the sun set from the beach. He would stroke my face with his big hands, like a child awkwardly petting a kitten and trying not to hurt it, and say things like "I always thought that if I met a beautiful and compatible woman my own age, it would be much better than being with a younger woman," or "Let's write a poem," or worst of all, "You would love Nice." He would quiz me on what had gone wrong with my relationships in the past, and was always touching me in public, as though saying, "Yes, she's with me!" Chameleon-like, I started to change.

When Cliff could see what I could not, that I was drifting into lovesick waters, he would remind me, "You aren't my girl-friend, you know, Miss Serial Mater." (He had Googled me, and the first thing he'd read was a quote from the earlier essay I had written in which I described myself as a "serial mater" versus a "serial dater," so he had been forewarned.) I would re-treat and say, "Of course not!" pretending that I still had some objectivity, but who was I really kidding?

It felt like I was in a tropical-vacation commercial, trying to tout the Fantasy Island Fling package to myself, complete with the attentive and handsome tour guide. The set looked good, but something was off, like I had been miscast in my own in-fomercial. Part of me didn't buy it, and I was starting to feel like I just wasn't right for this part. When I go to the movies, I have to suspend my disbelief long enough to enjoy the show, but in real life, where does reality end and fantasy begin? I was telling myself that this was just an experiment in sexual detachment for my vacation pleasure, but the truth is, I can't have sex with someone and not get attached. I don't know if it's a chemical thing or an attachment-disorder thing or a female thing. And it's probably a good thing, at least for me, so why do I keep pre-tending that it's not?

I guess reality ends and fantasy begins as soon as I decide that it's not okay just to be me.

Paul called for an update. "It sounds to me like you are try-ing to go left and right at the same time," he confirmed. "Quit trying to make Fling Guy into Relationship Guy!" And, taking his advice for once, I practiced detachment and didn't call Cliff for several days, instead preparing myself mentally to go home. By the time he finally did call, I was at the airport on my way back to California.

When I returned home, I braced myself not to hear from him but still hoped I would. And I did. It seemed my detach-ment had spurred him on, and we engaged in the modern-day equivalent of passing notes in homeroom via text messages and e-mail. One in particular said, "Remember, you are the kind of person that makes this world a great place to be hanging out. You're charming, beautiful, friendly, intelligent, tolerant, kind, sexy, and tall. Did I miss something? Your presence makes everything seem to be better. You have a certain magic quality. A shining light is your smile. You are always welcome at *chez moi*. I'm honored to be a part of your life. C."

Three thousand miles and the detachment of technology seemed like a safe enough distance for him to be intimate, and it started to feel like a cybercourtship. It may not have been real, but it was something.

When I described the situation to Rita, my therapist, the fol-lowing week, she reiterated something that I have heard her say before. "He's the classic dance-away lover. When you move forward, he moves back; when you move back, he moves for-ward." I considered this and asked, "Does this mean that I'm a classic dance-away lover, too? That I pick men who are un-available so that I don't have to look at my own unavailability?"

"How *would* you feel about being in a relationship with more substance?" she asked gently.

Feeling uncomfortable, I quipped, "Don't you remember? I'm a substance *abuser!*" but I knew that she was right. *Substance* seemed like such a dirty word to me, when all it really meant was that I was still afraid of anything real.

My laryngitis seemed a thing of the past, but since my body never lies, my acupuncturist, Stephen, noted, "Your body is working overtime to protect your heart, and it's stressing out your liver and lungs—what are you up to?"

Stephen had treated me for symptoms of perimenopause (basically feeling like a crazy, exhausted bitch) and had helped me completely turn my health around. He's an ex–Buddhist monk who loves to wear loud Hawaiian shirts (that his wife hates) and now sticks needles in people all day. He killed a mosquito during a recent session, and I asked, "What, you didn't want to usher him outside and set him free?" He replied, "No, he bit me earlier." I liked him for that.

Then he told me a story about when he was a monk in some tropical climate and couldn't wear insect repellent because of a bad rash. He had to experience mosquitoes biting him over and over while in meditation and do nothing about it except notice each one landing, then biting him, then sensations aris-ing. "Mosquitoes have taught me a lot, but I don't like to be bit," he said, flicking the dead insect off of his hand. Yeah, I know what you mean, I said to myself, thinking about some of the men I had dated.

I e-mailed pictures of Cliff playing Frisbee on the beach to my friend Jane, my fling expert friend, for her opinion. "He's hunky," she said, "but if it's just a fling, why are you still communicating with him? That's not sanctioned fling behavior."

"The fling's not over yet," I said. "I have one more trip to Maui scheduled for next month."

"Maybe there's more potential here with this one?" she said, ever the romantic at heart.

"Maybe," I said, trying to appear skeptical instead of hopeful. "We'll see."

and see we did, because as soon as I returned to Maui, things changed. Abruptly. Cliff started to mete out his attention, giving me just enough to keep me around but not enough to encourage me. He would ask me out and then be extremely passive and distant while we were together, letting me do all the work. He acted as though he had been set up on a date with an ugly long-removed cousin by his parents and couldn't wait for it to be over so he could go out and have real fun with his friends. "Listen," he said, "if I call you and you are available, great. But if not, it doesn't really matter to me. You are not my girlfriend, and none of this matters."

I know, I *know*! Right here is where I should have pulled the plug. I knew he was not my boyfriend, but fling or no fling, *I want to matter*. This was probably just his way of trying to end things, but since I was unwilling to accept this, I felt like I was in one of those Chinese finger puzzles; the more I struggled with the truth, the tighter the hold. This is where I get stuck, nonacceptance of what is. Intellectually I could see what was happening, but to little Wendy it was just inconceivable that Cliff would all of a sudden be so cold, and fear of abandonment set in. So, rather than just talking to him about how I felt, I resorted to a childhood coping mechanism—If I don't acknowledge something, then it doesn't have to be so—and went into denial about his actions. I redoubled my efforts to be fabulous and chose to believe that if I was pretty enough or charming enough or something enough that I could change his mind and get him to see how valuable I really was. *Then* it could be over.

This strategy resulted in Cliff's pressuring me to have a threesome, and an invitation to go to the sex clubs in Nice. His e-mails went from lovely to lewd. "You know what I love?" he started out, and my mind jumped to: "Me, of course!" He continued, "It's when Plato (my pit bull) licks my balls before I feed him. That's true love. A thing that you should take note of. So when's the next fuckfest, honey? Big C."

I knew that he was kidding—he didn't even have a dog—but I wasn't sure what was more horrifying to me, that he was saying these things or that I wasn't just telling him to shove it and moving on. But I felt so disappointed! I couldn't tell if he was a nice guy pretending to be a jerk, or a jerk pretending to be a nice guy. He should be voted "Aging jock trapped in a wounded child" in the yearbook of midlife, I thought, but what did that make me? Girl most likely to get her emotional ass kicked? Just how delusional was I?

Since this was not the first time I've had to ask myself this question in connection with some man, I continued to try to achieve perspective or at least some measure of sanity by being accountable for my behavior to my friends, hoping that eventually I'd learn how to be accountable to myself.

"Wendy, what do you expect? He's a jock!" Paul reminded me. "You never hear about some girl getting gang-raped by a team of chess players, do you? No, it's always the football team. Jocks stay immature jerks, they don't treat women with respect, and I'm going to kick his ass! You deserve better than this. Dump him immediately!"

He was right about one thing, I needed to let go, but I didn't want to know what I knew. Why can't I just be the worldly woman who can have flings and not get her feelings hurt? What is a fling anyway? I looked up *fling* in the dictionary:

fling *v*
1: to throw something or somebody fast using a lot of force
2: to jump forcefully in a way that seems impressive or dramatic, or to jump on somebody or something in the same way

3: to move your head or arms in a particular direction suddenly and dramatically

4: to start doing something with great enthusiasm and energy

fling *n [informal]*

1: a brief sexual relationship

2: a period of carefree enjoyment, especially before a more serious or worried period

Hmm, a brief sexual relationship where I dramatically and enthusiastically jump on somebody using excessive force, followed by a period of depression. That sounds about right. But wait, I signed up for this class. Where did I get the idea that this was desirable? What kind of degree was I going for? How many decisions in my life were being made based on ideas that I had about myself when I was thirteen?

When I hadn't heard from Cliff for a couple of days, I called him, more out of morbid curiosity than anything else. He was on his way to go snorkeling with a couple of new "friends."

"Do you want to come with us? I can pick you up—we are right near you," he said.

"Well, are these some girls that you picked up on the beach?" I asked, knowing the answer.

"Um, well, kind of, yes."

Silence.

"Well, maybe another time then," he said.

"Yeah, another time. See ya," I said.

"How much more information do you need?" Hedy asked as she confronted me still holding the dead phone in my hand. "This is classic passive–aggressive behavior—going from all sweetness and light to mean and ugly overnight, and then acting like nothing is wrong. Quit trying to make sense out of crazy!" she said, channeling Dr. Phil and hugging me tight.

By the end of the week, Cliff appeared to have lost interest in me completely and was openly flirting with other women in my presence. "I sure hope you're making a parachute out of all those red flags you've been collecting," Hedy said, minutes before I went to sit on Cliff's lap at a beach party of friends in a last-ditch attempt to get his attention. He leapt up as though I were a scalding cup of coffee and literally dumped me in the sand.

Feeling like a bird that had just fallen off its perch and trying to look casual about it, I picked myself up and walked back to the house to go hide in yet another bathroom. I hadn't seen this much bathroom action since I was bulimic. What was I doing?

Closing the bathroom door, I brushed the sand off my skirt, took a deep breath, and tried to settle down and really listen to what my body was saying. I wasn't even sure I liked this guy, so why did I feel so hurt?

I remembered when I was fourteen and had gotten really drunk for the first time by downing eight Budweiser beers in an hour. I was with some friends at a motorcycle race, and an older boy, Johnny, asked me to push his dirt bike so he could get it started. Thrilled to have been asked, I gripped his seat from behind and started pushing. What Johnny had neglected to tell me was when to let go. So as the bike kicked into gear, I held on, and wanting to be sure to do it just right, I was dragged for about ten feet before it even occurred to me to let go. What I wanted was Johnny's approval. What I got was face-down drunk in the dirt.

With Cliff, I'd told myself I wanted a fling. What I got was flung. But who had really done the flinging?

I looked into the bathroom mirror for that sweet little seventh-grade girl who wanted so much to get on the dance floor with the prom king and who wasn't at all prepared to end up in this mosh pit.

"Who knew that the prom king was going to turn out to be such an asshole?" I said out loud to myself, trying to make little Wendy feel better.

But I knew it was much more than that. The problem was not him, it was me. And the solution lay in taking responsibility for myself. Surrender or be dragged. This was my doing, and it would be my undoing unless I could let go and accept the situation for what it was. Which was over or, if I was being truthful with myself, a nonstarter. If succeeding in the art of the fling meant remaining emotionally detached, clearly I had failed. But maybe what seemed like failure was really progress. Or, as Thomas Edison said, "I have not failed. I've just found ten thousand ways that won't work."

I finally came out of the bathroom (a small line had formed), feeling better than I had in weeks. Determined to find Hedy and make my way home, I was intercepted by the tall, gorgeous musician who had provided the earlier background music to my Cliff diving. At first he looked so stricken and tongue-tied that I thought he might be on his way to the bathroom to throw up. But as I started to walk around him, he touched my arm, and a bolt of electricity shot through me.

"Hi," he sputtered. "I wanted to meet you."

"Hi," I said, and reached out to shake his hand. I smiled and thought, Could this be the shy, previously dorky musician guy from band that I never got to date in high school? As I gazed into his appreciative eyes, I suddenly had an idea. Maybe he sees me as the tall, thin, foxy blonde he never got to date in high school. Maybe we are *all* just walking around in various states of confusion and delusion, some part of us forever underage. Maybe high school never really leaves us, but we can learn to leave it. Maybe I'll never really grow up, but maybe, just maybe, I can get better at being young as I grow old. I may have been temporarily blinded by the glare of Cliff's flashlight, but at least I finally saw the light, my light. As James Thurber said, "There are two kinds of light—the glow that illuminates, and the glare that obscures," and suddenly, feeling lit from within, I felt the sun rise in my very own Emerald City–green eyes.

THE WISDOM OF
MEN-O-PAUSE

last year my three younger sisters all chipped in to give me a special gift for my birthday. I *love* getting presents, so when I received their box in the mail, I immediately sat down and ripped it open. Inside I found a tastefully wrapped basket containing a book, *The Wisdom of Menopause,* a certificate to join a popular dating service, and two jars of face cream, one for daytime use called Hope in a Jar, and the other a night cream called When Hope Is Not Enough.

Also enclosed was a sympathy card expressing deep regret at the passing of my youth and a pretty but *very* conservative beige sweater set (you know, the kind you might see Barbara Bush wearing) that was several sizes too large.

Now, I know the basket was a joke. But since I am the oldest and in my forties, and my sisters are all more or less married, I couldn't help but hear, "You are getting old and fat and will die alone if you don't get moving. Use it or lose it, sister!"

Thanks, girls! I said to myself as I held the sweater set up to my chest, studied my reflection in a nearby mirror, and frowned. The only thing missing is a tasteful strand of pearls, I thought, and lightly touching my collarbones, remembered when getting a "pearl necklace" had a com*pletely* different meaning. Turning away from the mirror, I wondered why all of a sudden getting another year older seemed so hard.

Granted, it is possible that I was a little overly sensitive about aging at the time, having been recently dumped by a younger man because, as he put it, "your eggs are no longer viable." Although my girlfriend Cameron pointed out that "when they start saying your *legs* are no longer viable, that's when you need to worry," I swear his comment threw me into peri-menopause. I had accepted the idea that I would never bear children, but I had never been rejected by a man because of my inability to conceive. I was starting to feel like I had been left on the shelf past my expiration date.

Hadn't this been the objective for most of my single life, to enjoy sex and not get pregnant? I had breezed through my thirtieth and fortieth birthdays, wondering what all the fuss was about. My biological clock may have been ticking all along, but I finally got alarmed. I may not have children, but I don't want to be rejected because I can't!

Fears about menopause aside, I've never been a sweater-set girl (and certainly did not want to be mistaken for a

Republican), so I would later return the sweaters to Macy's "Past Her Prime" department and exchange them for sexy lingerie and a trendy lime-green skirt. I may be living in denial of my age, but as long as I can get away with wearing a thong, I will. Plus, being single again meant that I could buy underwear with impunity, since it has been my experience that buying lingerie when I'm actually dating someone seems to be the kiss of death—a certain precursor to breaking up. (Also included in this superstitious category is leaving something that I care about at his house, making long-term vacation plans, and shaving my underarms in front of him.) I don't, however, want to end up being fifty years old trying to look like I'm still twenty-five, so I have a trusted stylist friend who has promised to let me know if and when I cross that fine line and to usher me into my age group.

As for the rest of the basket, I put the creams and dating-service certificate aside (for now) and sat down to read *The Wisdom of Menopause*. At first it seemed overwhelmingly negative and absolutely terrifying—horror-monal stories of weight gain, night sweats, and mood swings—but as I dug a little deeper, I found a chapter with a shred of hope. Apparently all of these symptoms were labor pains leading up to a birth—or a rebirth—of me. It seems that the biggest promise of getting through "the change" was that my brain chemistry will change and I will finally have more access to my intuitive, higher self. Perhaps the sane, calm, and knowing woman who had appeared in my life only periodically would now become a regular, even as my periods became irregular. This saner version of me had previously been only a sidekick in my life—the dependable Ed McMahon to my chronically irreverent Johnny Carson or the likable Andy to my unpredictable Conan—and I was looking forward to her taking on a bigger part of the show.

Anyway, the idea that I will have more clarity and focus, and be able to use my intuition on a regular basis instead of constantly being at the mercy of my hormones, was appealing. Losing the elasticity of my skin and interest in sex was not.

A few months later, my up-and-coming intuitive cohost made an appearance in the form of a bad joke during sex. While clearly still at the mercy of my hormones, I was making love with Ken, yet another younger and inappropriate but sexy boyfriend. His penis was very hard, and I stroked it teasingly. "Wow, did you take Viagra, or are you just really glad to see me?" I asked.

Ken had always used the state of his penis as a barometer of his attraction to me, often taking my hand and pushing it against his crotch when we would meet to show me the effect I was having on him. He seemed inordinately proud of his erections, and sexual chemistry had been an important part of our equation, or so I thought!

He looked sort of shocked, then sheepish, and stammered, "Well, yes, I did. And I guess . . . I mean, I am, glad to see you."

My hand stopped midstroke as I absorbed what he was saying. I was kidding about the Viagra; he was only forty years old!

I closed my eyes for a second. This explains so much, I

thought. It was as though an important and elusive centerpiece of the jigsaw puzzle that was Ken had suddenly dropped into place, and a whole new version of our relationship emerged in my mind.

I remembered some talk-show psychologist warning that "in bed with someone's penis in your hand" was not the ideal place to discuss sexual dysfunction. But there I was, penis in hand, about to plunge into dangerous territory. My head was reeling with questions. Why had he taken it? Was it me? Did he take it to get a hard-on or keep one? I wasn't very well versed in Viagra and assumed that dating younger men meant that I wouldn't have to be for at least a few more years. (Thanks to my seventeen years in recovery from alcoholism, forced clean living, and my emotional immaturity, I seem younger than I am and tend to attract younger men. I felt I had made some progress in discernment by ruling out anyone who called me "dude," wore chains on his belt, or overused expressions like "Sweet!" to describe something he liked, but Ken had somehow slipped through the screening cracks.)

I opened my eyes and proceeded with caution. "Is this something that you take all the time?" I asked, not really sure I wanted to hear the answer, and even less sure what to do with my hand.

"Um, yes," he said nervously.

"What, like every time we've made love?" I said, my mind racing back over the past few months.

"Pretty much," he replied.

"Why?" I asked, wondering if he had needed to take Viagra with Victoria, his beautiful ex-girlfriend.

"Ever since I got sober," he answered, "my equipment has been . . . unreliable. It doesn't matter who I'm with. Sometimes it works, but most of the time it doesn't. When I smoked pot, I could fuck all night and not lose my erection, but without it, well, it's a problem."

Fuck.

Fortunately, I was seeing my therapist the next day, so I took my unanswered Viagra questions to Rita. Rita had been my therapist for about a year, and we had been working on how I could take the "me" out of men—no small feat. I had been in a series of co-dependent and inappropriate relationships, and I didn't want to continue to do the same thing over and over again, expecting different results. (Maybe what I should really have asked myself was when was I going to be able to take the men out of me!)

"Viagra?! I know it's not all about me, but what about me?" I asked defensively, flopping down on the couch for our session, deciding that if it couldn't be all about me in therapy, where could it? As I described the Viagra incident in question, Rita grabbed her copy of the *Physicians' Desk Reference* (something all good therapists and recovering drug addicts are familiar with), and together we reviewed the indications and side effects of the drug.

"Okay," she said, flipping through the heavy book to the V's, "it says that men take Viagra about an hour before they want to have sex." She read a little more. "The gist of it seems to be that Viagra doesn't cause the penis to become erect but keeps it in play once it's there."

"Good, so at least that means he's still probably attracted to me," I said, "but does it make it harder for him to come?"

Rita replied, "Yes, it's harder for him to come."

Well, that explains a few things, I thought, unconsciously rubbing the sore muscles in my jaw.

This may have been my first experience with Viagra, but it was certainly not my first experience with sexually dysfunctional men. I crossed and uncrossed my legs, gearing up to rationalize my choices, and said, "You know, he really took a chance telling me the truth, he could easily have lied." I continued, picking up steam, "Maybe he's becoming the real *stand-up* guy I'm looking for who's finally *coming* around and taking a *hard* look at himself," I said, using my trusty and battered pun shield to deflect any real feelings.

Rita looked at me with her loving, steady gaze and, smiling gently, said, "That reminds me, have you heard about the new Viagra eyedrops that make you take a hard look at yourself? Why don't I write you a prescription?"

I sighed, wishing my healthier coping skills were as strong as my denial. "Good idea," I said. "Better make it an endless refill."

Driving home from my session, I reflected that maybe Ken's using Viagra to maintain his erection was not that much different from me faking the occasional orgasm. I mean, wasn't I sometimes faking it just to further excite my lover, equating his hard-on with my self-worth? Maybe erections are just as important to a woman's self-esteem as they are to a man's. If I were a man and had trouble maintaining an erection, what would I do, aside from everything I could possibly think of, including therapy, hypnotism, acupuncture, taking herbs like Ram Goat Dash Along or Horny Goat Weed, eating oysters, drinking tequila, watching porn, and dating twenty-five-year-olds? (Yikes, that was scary, I felt like I was inside of a man's head there for a minute!) Since men can't fake an erection, I wonder if impotence is the male version of men-o-pause?

I have never told any of the men I've been with when I've staged an orgasm and certainly no one has ever asked (apparently I'm convincing). I mean, who asks a question that they really don't want answered (aside from me)? Sometimes I fake it because I don't want to inspire hurt feelings, or I'm tired and want to get it over with, or I'm just trying to "fake it until I make it." But other times I'm just afraid—afraid to tell the truth, especially in the bedroom. How hard would it be to just say, "I'm sorry, I can't come right now. I'm tired, I feel emotionally detached from you, none of my backup fantasies are working, and just getting off with your penis is impossible right now, so can you please just finish up and let's get some sleep!"

God, no wonder men are using Viagra!

In the end, maybe relationships and menopause are like the labor pains of childbirth. Denial is key to getting into them and through them, and what keeps us going through all the pain and fear is a promise, the promise of a birth: of a child, a new love, or even a new me. And maybe my denial is just optimism dressed in black, and all that really matters is how well I treat myself and other people in the process.

When I got home that evening, I listened to a message on my answering machine from my sister Vicki while I was dressing to go out on a dinner date with a girlfriend. Afterward, we were planning on checking out a new show in town called *Menopause: The Musical.*

"Hey, Wen, if you liked what we got you for your birthday last year," she said, "you are going to love what we're planning for your next one. . . ." And as she continued alluding to this year's evil surprise, I went to my closet and put on my birthday thong and trendy lime-green skirt, sauntered over to the dresser, where I applied just a little Hope, and this time when I caught my reflection in the mirror, I smiled.

Maybe I was living and finally learning, after all!

Famous last words . . .

STILL BORN

god, i hate this night. I've stayed put, waiting for him to call. We've been dating for four months. Earlier in the day he said he would call after work. He's been pulling away and standoffish the past two weeks, and I really want to feel connected again. I feel him slipping away. I try to pretend I don't care.

I start feeling anxious about nine-fifteen. What time does he get off work tonight? Probably about ten. No problem, he'll probably call me around ten-fifteen. At nine-thirty I take a shower, soften my skin, wait. I clean the bathroom. I watch TV.

At ten-thirty, visions of other women start dancing in my head, and I feel panicky. I don't want to know what I know. I don't want to let go, but I have rope burns from holding on. The pain of holding on is almost greater than the pain of letting go, but not quite. I'm still attached. I don't want to feel this pain. I don't want to be this upset. I want to stay in the illusion of this love affair, but I knew this day would come. It would be so much easier just to blame him. His behavior has been outrageous. But I know that it's me. My choice. I created this situation for myself. *But why?*

I call him at eleven, getting his machine. "Are you still working? Come over, I want you!" I try to sound casual. This relationship was supposed to stay casual. But I do not sound casual. It did not stay casual. I am embarrassed by the intensity of my desire for him. I curl my bangs. I apply blush. I brush my teeth. Dab on perfume.

It's eleven-fifteen. I text-message him, *What up?* No response. I sand my feet and file my nails. I brush my teeth again. I watch the clock in five-minute intervals. My hope flickers like a self-extinguishing flame. I alternate between feeling self-righteous and needy.

At midnight I try phoning again. I try to keep my tone low and reasonable, but I feel betrayed. "I get that you aren't coming over, but you know how you sometimes call and call me when you can't reach me and wonder where I am when you really need to talk? Well, now it's my turn. I guess I really just needed you tonight. Please call me. I'm awake."

I watch myself pace between the living room and kitchen, then to the bathroom, opening and closing drawers, never standing still, waiting tensely for something to happen. Waiting for him to call. The after-midnight terrors that I used to experience in early sobriety some seventeen years ago start creeping in. My mind is a smoky, crowded bar in a bad neighborhood, and everyone is drunk and shouting, "HE'S WITH ANOTHER WOMAN. IT'S OVER. YOU WILL NEVER BE TOGETHER AGAIN. HE'S LIED TO YOU THIS WHOLE TIME. YOU AREN'T ENOUGH. YOU SHOULD HAVE KNOWN BETTER, AND NOW HE'S LEAVING YOU!" I know in my gut that everyone is right.

Two a.m. I know he's not coming over. I know he's not going to call. I picture him dead at the side of the road. It doesn't help. I keep moving things around, silly things—my sunglasses, my iPod, a stack of papers—trying to initiate order. I put a box of Kleenex and some massage oil near the bed as though he were still coming. I go into the bathroom and stare at myself in the mirror. I realize that the blush I put on earlier was not blush but purple eye shadow. I anxiously pick my face. I can't believe he's not calling me back! How could he do this to *me*! Suddenly I am so angry that I don't know what to do. I start to shake and feel sick and grip the bathroom counter. I feel like I've been on heavy-duty pain medication for a chronic condition and it's starting to wear off. I want to do something that will bring me relief, but there is nothing left to do. I am at odds with myself. I want to find him and make this different, and I know I cannot. I must accept what is happening, but I will not. I feel dizzy with conflicting desires. To control and to release. To render and to destroy. Withholding myself from myself. Anorexic spirit. Bombarded with grief. So angry and so betrayed. Forces of opposition are killing me. This feeling is excruciating. I can't tell if it's a prolonged death or a slow birth. *What's wrong with me?*

I stare at my reflection. I see Glenn Close in *Fatal Attraction.* You are acting crazy, I think. You are a grown woman; get a grip. Then I realize that I'm not a grown woman, not right now. I am a child right now, a rejected child. Why did this have to happen today? I don't want to feel this *today.* I go out to the patio and smoke. I rip the filter off my cigarette and feel the smoke burn my lungs. I want to feel something, anything, other than crazy. I go back to the bathroom, brush my teeth for the tenth time, wash my hands. I am trying to outdistance this pain, but nothing helps. I feel mentally ill. I wring my clean hands. Back in the living room, I glance at the TV and see the OCD detective Monk. Perfect. I change the channel. A made-for-TV movie involving group sex. I change the channel. A man betrays his lover. I change the channel. A movie I've seen before with a middle-aged Patricia Clarkson, drunk and despairing, abandoned by her lover. Change the channel. A woman in a straitjacket who is tied down to a gurney and screaming.

I sit on the couch and mute the TV. I stare at the images moving across the screen. I'm having trouble differentiating between reality and my fear. I know my perception is distorted. I can't accept any version of my story. Every channel in my head is a nightmare. I fold my hands across my heart and grip my arms like I am cold and bend over to rest my purple cheek on my knees. My therapist, Rita, says that when I can hold opposing emotions without acting out, that's a sign of emotional maturity, and wisdom follows. I pretend that I have emotional maturity. I close my eyes and try to visualize what is happening to me.

I am in a rented blue two-door Hyundai, lost in a scary neighborhood in the dead of night without directions. I have been driving in circles. I'm anxiously waiting at a stoplight. I have déjà vu. Where am I? I look up at the street sign. I am at the intersection of Illusion and Reality. *Fuck!* How did I get *here*? I lock my door. I fiddle with the radio. Suddenly, in my rearview mirror, I see a Mack truck barreling down on me at seventy miles per hour. The headlights blind me. In a few seconds I know I will be hit. I can see the collision happening, and there is nothing that I can do to stop it. I am filled with dread. Why is this so familiar? I have never been in a car accident. This is not a literal event. What does it represent? I jerk up out of the exercise. This is not helping, but the feeling persists. I know what this is. I have been here before, at this particular intersection in fact, on this same day, January 19, so many years ago.

I brace myself for the impact. They say in Al-Anon that feeling your feelings leads to freedom, but I think feeling my feelings leads to death. Maybe it's the same thing.

I pull my mind back to HIM. I thought I could control my emotions around this affair, but I could not. I want him to come over and hold me and tell me that everything will be okay. But he will not. I want to be enough for him. I am not. I want him to want me the way he did in the beginning. He does not. Intellectually I know that right now HE just represents every love loss, every betrayal—that it's not really about him. He did not cause this. He cannot fix this. But my heart is breaking and my arms and legs start burning with something like shame, and my hands shake. I am reminded of why I drank. I feel like I'm falling, and I'm scared. My body remembers, I think. My body always remembers, even when I try to forget. I struggle not to cry and focus instead on my breath, in and out, in and out. I rock backward and forward on the couch in my seated fetal position. "Please help me," I whisper. "Please help me," and I listen, and I wait, and I breathe.

After a while, a gentle knowing says, *Go ahead and surrender,* and tears spring to my eyes. I don't want to. It continues, *There is nothing else to do. You are loved, and I am here.* I hug myself, rubbing my hands up and down my arms. *Go ahead and remember, it's going to be okay.* I don't believe this. Truisms start running through my head, like *Whatever you resist persists* and *Surrender means going over to the winning side* and *Whenever I argue with what is, I lose.* I hate these sayings and resent that this gentle knowing has chosen to use clichés in my time of need, but I am desperate now, so I let them in. There is nothing left to do tonight but feel my feelings. I know that I cannot drink or smoke or snort or eat or fuck or joke or buy my way out of this. There is a different price to be paid. Nothing else works anymore. *You won't die,* I remind myself, *it wasn't you that died.* But I know I will. Part of me will. Part of me always does. Feel and remember, I think, and lower myself onto the couch and hold still.

my mother was never still, and even when she wasn't moving, she seemed to vibrate and rev, like an engine impatiently idling at a longer-than-usual stoplight. She fueled herself with organic foods, growing her own bean sprouts and making her own yogurt long before it was trendy, and believed that good nutrition would inevitably lead to happiness.

"Do you see this tooth?" she asked one day when I was about eight years old. "The tooth fairy dropped it off so that I could show you what sugar does to your teeth," she said, dropping what looked suspiciously like my latest molar into the glass of Coke—something absolutely forbidden in our household. "Just think what it does to your insides," she warned as my three little sisters and I watched with morbid fascination over the next week while the tooth slowly dissolved, a stream of carbonation escorting it into oblivion. More than anything, this made me want to drink Coke until my head exploded.

My mother's approach to nutrition had afforded her a beautiful veneer. She was petite and curvaceous, with short, curly auburn hair, and I always imagined that she could have been Elizabeth Taylor's younger brown-eyed sister. I felt proud of how beautiful she was, but her eyes were always tense, as though she was bracing herself against the next moment. I remember looking up at her in the grocery store, the Co-op in Berkeley, where we shopped for the week's healthy groceries every Saturday morning, her face tight as she awkwardly held her hand out waiting for change from the cashier. I wanted to say, *Mommy, can't you just relax and be happy?* and I felt embarrassed by her inability to be at home in the world.

My mother liked having babies. I was her firstborn, or "the experimental model," as my father called me, and was followed by my little sisters, Vicki, Robin, and Christina, in rapid succession. As long as she had a newborn child in her arms she seemed content. She was a children's librarian and always wanted a little boy so that she could name him Christopher Robin, a *Winnie-the-Pooh* character, but she had to settle for a Christina and a Robin instead. I'm not sure where the name Vicki came from, but I know I was her Wendy from *Peter Pan*.

Watching us get older was difficult for her. She seemed both to lament and encourage our growth. She always complained, "My babies are growing up too fast!" Yet when I was three years old and asked to drink her coffee, she said, "If you drink coffee, then you won't grow up big and strong." To which I replied, "I thought you didn't want your babies to grow up!"

At the same time, I felt rushed to mature. "As soon as you can reach this shelf, I want you to start folding your own laundry," she said, pointing to the plastic bins with our names on them that lay in waiting above the washer and dryer in our garage. I was nine years old, and although folding laundry hardly seemed like an incentive to grow up, I felt anxious about being able to do things for myself. "It's important that you learn to be independent," she said, as though preparing me for her early departure.

My mother was very artsy and had converted a big closet in our hallway into a craft room filled with projects for her school library. She had a kiln, and glue guns, and knickknacks galore, and I vividly remember the plaster-of-Paris Medusa she made with dozens of tiny rubber snakes jutting out of its head, which seemed so real, I halfway believed the legend that if I looked directly at her, I would be turned to stone. My mom created a magical alternate reality of puppets and games and stories in this room, and I felt safe as long as I was in it.

When she wasn't melting something in her kiln, or writing children's books, or knitting my father a tie, or braiding a rug, or making puppets, or watching Julia Child, or practicing guitar, or baking a complicated birthday cake that she would later construct into a series of barnyard animals (consisting, naturally, of whole-wheat flour, wheat germ, and cream-cheese frosting), she was sewing her own clothes, which ranged from knitted dresses to leopard headbands to the capri pants popular in the sixties.

No, my mother never seemed to stop moving, as though if she did, even for a second, she would be overtaken by a gigantic tsunami and swept away. And eventually, well, eventually that's exactly what happened.

She stopped being able to hide her depression when I was about twelve. She had been in therapy for about a year before she told my father. She seemed like a bird that was afraid that if she were found sick, she would be kicked out of the nest. Doctors eventually treated her depression with shock therapy, believing that if her mind could be erased, then she would forget why she was unhappy. And it worked, for a while. But she also forgot who we were, and as her memory of us returned, so did the depression.

I was never sure whether she would be okay or not when I got home from school. Sometimes she was in the kitchen baking oatmeal-raisin cookies, or vacuuming the seventies shag carpet in the living room, or practicing tai chi, and everything seemed fine. Other times I would find her lying on the shag carpet in the living room, sobbing, as though she had simply dropped from her perch, unable to go on. I became watchful of her eyes and learned to anticipate her moods. If I could make her laugh, I was exulted. But making her mad was okay, too. Anything real was better than nothing at all.

I got good at provoking her and once made her so mad that she started to choke me. Another time she threw a handful of cutlery at me before bursting into tears. She had a short fuse, so I learned how to light it and run. My little sister Tina wasn't as fast and often got her mouth washed out with paprika.

Each year in June, I would ask my mother, "What do you want for your birthday?" hoping to be able to give her something, anything, that would make her happy. "I just want four good little girls," she would say, and my heart would sink, knowing I could only disappoint her.

When I was sixteen, she came home from the school library, put a ham in the oven for our dinner, went upstairs to her bedroom, and took an overdose of pills. She must have gotten scared or changed her mind, because after a little while, she called my dad and told him what she had done. Then she put me on the phone with him.

"Your mother has taken an overdose," he said flatly. "Stay with her and wait for the ambulance." I had been home sick that day with strep throat, and my voice was hoarse and my head throbbed with fever.

I ran upstairs where she had retreated to her bedroom and found her standing in the doorway, holding on to each side of the doorframe, as though she was experiencing an earthquake. My three little sisters stood around her, clinging to her, crying.

"Mommy Mommy Mommy," my sister Tina wailed. She was nine years old, the youngest, and the most intuitive of the four of us. In the last few years, my mother had clung to her like a life raft. "My babies are all growing up," she would wail, pulling Tina into her lap at the dinner table and bursting into tears.

Now she rocked back and forth, side to side, moaning, "I'm so sorry, I'm so sorry, this is going to scar you for the rest of your lives. I'm so sorry, this is going to scar you for the rest of your lives, my babies, my babies. How could I leave my babies?" She seemed to be speaking not to us but to middle space, and her eyes looked like they had been recently repossessed.

I stood across the hall from my mother, mirroring her in the doorframe of my own bedroom, watching her grip the wood frame for dear life. She was only three feet away, but the distance felt insurmountable, feverishly surreal, and inside my head I screamed, *THAT'S RIGHT. HOW COULD YOU LEAVE YOUR BABIES? DON'T DO THIS, MOMMY. DON'T LEAVE US. PLEASE DON'T GO. HOW COULD YOU DO THIS? DON'T YOU LOVE US? WHY ARE YOU DOING THIS? PLEASE DON'T GO!*

I HATED her and LOVED her, and the forces of opposition were so unbearable that I blacked out with rage as I watched my sisters cling to her arms and legs, weeping, everyone weeping now except me, who stood there, fuming and shaking and sixteen and sick and furious.

The ambulance finally came, and the driver led her away as she wrung her hands, repeating over and over, "I'm so sorry, I'm so sorry, this is going to scar you for the rest of your lives, I'm so sorry ..."

I struggled to maintain control. "She's going to be all right," I told my sisters, but Tina was sobbing, repeating again and again, "She's never coming back, she's never coming back ..."

Later, in the hospital, my mother's brain exploded. "They didn't pump her stomach," my father told me. "They said they needed to operate on her brain to relieve the pressure, and she had a cerebral hemorrhage. She's a vegetable, but they are keeping her alive on life support." He added, almost as an afterthought, "Her last words were, 'I can't leave my babies ...' "

Alone in my room, I begged God to let her live. *Please don't take her,* I cried. *Please, please let her live. I don't care if she's a vegetable; I'll take care of her. Please, God, help us, help my mother. Please don't let her leave us!* I cried and cried and broke and bled as I offered myself on the altar of my mother's shame. *PLEASE, GOD, I'LL DO ANYTHING. PLEASE DON'T TAKE MY MOTHER. PLEASE FORGIVE HER. PLEASE LET HER STAY. LET ME LOVE HER. LET THAT BE ENOUGH. PLEASE DON'T LET HER DIE!*

It was the last time I would cry for many years.

I remember the moment, the next day, January 19, as I was walking up the staircase from our living room when I heard my father on the phone, talking with the hospital. "You might just as well pull the plug," he said. "As far as I'm concerned, she checked out two days ago."

I froze, gripping the banister. I looked down at the blue-and-green wall-to-wall shag carpet that my mother just loved, and the matching blue peacock wall clock that she had created by smashing Noxzema jars into smithereens and melting the shards in her kiln. She had glued the smooth little chips of melted glass onto a clock face, and for some reason that I never understood but that somehow made perfect sense to her, she had stuck a jeweled peacock pin amid the broken glass. I focused on the peacock's glittering eye, and everything was bright and quiet, and I heard myself exhale. As I took my next breath, the burning wick of my father's words set off an explosion in my head, and I dropped to my knees on the stairs. Centrifugal force seemed to pull me away from the moment, and I watched from a growing distance as the picture of life as I knew it was shattered. In one horrible instant, I took in the truth, a sixteen-year-old child's truth of what was happening, and I started falling. I braced myself for the impact.

Within two weeks, I was smoking pot or drinking almost every day.

Within a month, I was anorexic and then bulimic.

Within three months, my married thirty-five-year-old boss was on top of me trying to fuck me.

b a c k   i n   m y living room, it's the darkest time of night, right before dawn. I am crying now, there is no stopping these tears. I am so tired of being strong. I feel so all alone. I know he has chosen to be with another woman, and it's like I am there, witnessing the betrayal. I cannot pull away from this image, and it extorts my grief. My body burns with adrenaline, and my mind races back and forth between the present and the past until they converge.

I cry out, *What did I do wrong!?* (*Mommee, I'll be good!*)

How could you do this to me!? (*I need youuu!*)

Choose me! (*Nooo, Mommeee, don't gooo!!*)

Why can't I be enough!? (*WHY CAN'T YOU LIVE FOR MEEE!!?*)

Love me! (*LOVE MEEE!!*)

I feel rejected and ashamed. I am humiliation. I am grief. I am freaking out. I have used this man to rip open a wound. How many times must I relive this? Are all my relationships *still in reaction to this*?

I let myself sob like the heartbroken child that I am. I cannot outdistance this pain. I stop struggling. I stop fighting. There is no escape. After a while, my sobs subside. I am strangely calm. The gentle knowing is here, just beyond my grief. I raise my arms straight up above my head and say, *UP, UP*, a small child asking to be picked up by a loving mother. I reach for the embrace that I am longing for. I imagine being lifted into loving arms and held and rocked and cuddled. I imagine being safe. I imagine being enough. I hear, *It's okay, sweetie. I'm here. You aren't alone.* I allow myself to feel loved. Part of me is screaming, *What kind of New Age airy-fairy bullshit is this? You are in the middle of being rejected by HIM. You are a loser, and*... But the power that these thoughts have over me is fading. For this moment I can let go of him. I can let her be. I stop gripping. I cease to fall. I have had enough for now. I will be enough for now. I turn my attention toward the love. For now I choose Love. I am Love. I roll over on my side and rub my arm, stroke my hair ... a mother now, comforting her distraught child. I start to relax. The tidal wave recedes. Part of me has washed away, but I am still here. I lay quietly in the breaking dawn, and lulled by the soft sound of my breath, the steady beat of my heart, I drift off to sleep in the arms of my beloved.

And I am, still.

ART THERAPY

not long afterward, while cleaning house, I absently dusted the surface of a painting that my ex-husband had given me, when it suddenly smashed to the ground and dislodged from its frame. Startled out of my daydreaming, I leaned down to pick it up and assess the damage. I wondered if this was a sign. I had become a big fan of paying attention to the things in my daily life that called attention to themselves. My paintings were the only things, aside from my eternal baggage, that I had carried from one phase of my life to the next. I had grown so accustomed to my collection that I rarely saw the pictures hanging on my walls anymore. My ex-husband and I had been divorced for a long time now. I wondered what, if anything, this meant.

I picked up the painting to take a closer look. It was an abstract, with vibrant orange and blue hues, of a solitary woman in repose, her hands behind her head, Picasso-like breasts falling out of her low-cut blouse. I peered at her for a few minutes, until another picture started to emerge. Was she resting on her hands, or were they tied behind her head? I studied it. Could be either way. How odd. I looked into her eyes. I had always thought she looked rather pleased with herself, but now she looked different. Still beautiful but remote, like a vacant property with lots of curb appeal. Pure potential. Daring me to untie her hands and let her show me what she could do. Untapped. Trapped. Oil, waiting to be discovered.

This painting had been hanging in my bedroom for years.

I started to feel uncomfortable. I reflected for a moment about the woman I had been when I received this gift for my birthday some ten years ago. My ex had been very generous but usually gave me gifts that he himself liked: art, jewelry, clothing. He was an architect and a fine artist himself, with excellent taste, but Svengali-like, he rarely took into consideration my preferences. Although to be fair, my preferences were unknown to me at that point in my life. I was more like tofu, assuming the flavor of whatever I was marinating in, and tended to let my husband take responsibility for many of my decisions so that I didn't have to. I had learned much about the world of art and design and fashion from him, but had I ever really considered whether or not I liked this painting? It was perceived as valuable, so I had held on to it, but what value did it really have to me now? Did I want to live with the woman in this painting today? Was I the woman in this painting? Was my art a reflection of my life, or my life a reflection of my art? And what else did I have hanging on my walls?

Curious now, I put the broken painting aside and, feather duster in hand, surveyed the bedroom walls. The largest piece in the room was a watercolor abstract of a nude woman painted on architectural blueprints instead of canvas. I had been irresistibly drawn to this painting and had purchased it on my own, without my husband's blessing, in what was to be the last year of our marriage. Several years later, I noticed the words "No Exit" buried deep within the abstraction. At the time, I thought this ironic, but as I looked at the painting now, I noticed something that I had never seen before: A tiny, devastatingly grief-stricken face emerged from behind the larger nude, and she looked so hopeless that tears sprang to my eyes. How was it that I had never seen this before? Was this woman hidden beneath my surface as well? Did I really want this grief-stricken woman in my bedroom? What if these paintings were acting as mirrors, reflecting my past into my future? I took the painting down and put it with the other.

I continued into the living room. A huge oil portrait that my friend Vanya had painted portrayed me as a sea goddess from another world, another life, holding a conch shell at my belly with both hands, straddling my seat, my white robe falling open around my shoulders. In it, I am looking away from the viewer over my right shoulder toward the distant horizon of ocean in the background. The painting was titled *Assignation with Nemo.* The woman in the painting was strong, but Vanya had also captured an intense, vulnerable quality of elusiveness and longing that was hard to look at. This trend was disturbing. Who was this woman, trapped in a solitary state of waiting, for lifetimes? Was this to be her past, present, and future state of being? What, or whom, was she waiting for?

I looked around my living room at the rest of the paintings. Another moody sepia-toned oil painting of me by Vanya. A surreal naked lightbulb illuminating a vacant chair. A large canvas with multiple takes of a single pear, seen over and over again from different angles. An abstract of a woman, nose pressed against the glass of a window, wistfully gazing at the colorful fruit inside. In another, a serene woman, eyes closed, hair streaming out behind her as though she were floating. Or high. Or dead. *Oh my God,* this was getting worse and worse! I have surrounded myself with visions of mysterious obscurity. Enigmatic, ethereal epigrams. My living room feels as though it been waiting for eons, like a lost continent, to be discovered. Virgin soiled. Was this a reflection of my life or driving my state of being? One by one, I took the pictures down.

I proceeded to the bathroom. A few years ago, I had come across a box of drawings that I had done as a little girl. As a demonstration of the reclamation of that little girl and in the

spirit of a mother hanging her child's drawings on the refrigerator (and at the recommendation of my therapist), I had
mounted a few of them and hung them in the bathroom. I
looked at them now. A little girl, reading, sprawled across a
multicolored beach towel. A paper cutout of a lion, smiling,
sitting alone. A solitary bunny, poised, listening. Fragments.
Flashbacks. Had I always seen myself alone? Another
portrayed a mother duck, leading her baby chicks across a dangerous crowded street to a toy store on the other side, everybody quacking and honking. It seemed both ominous and
sweet. Like my childhood.

I moved into my office. Here I had framed several photos
of myself at different stages of my life. In one, I was five
years old, posing in a puffy little dress, patent-leather shoes,
peeking out shyly from beneath my bangs, trying to stand perfectly straight. A black-and-white eight-by-ten close-up showed
my unmarred sixteen-year-old face staring boldly into the reflective lens, a photo taken just months before my mother was
to die. Another from my twenties, the pretend party girl, eyes
closed, smiling. Sort of. A shot from my thirties, back to the
camera, silk sarong–waisted, hanging loosely from a long
tree limb stretched over the shallow waters of a Hawaiian shore.
Toe surfing. I wanted these girls, this woman, to be cared for,
and had put the photos in my office to remind me of who I was
working to support.

Hanging above my computer was a painting by Medora, a

woman who had been like a surrogate mother to me. Her daughter had died the same way my mother had. We cobbled together. Her style was abstract realism, and this painting represented Medora at various stages in her life. Dominated by men, pushing a baby carriage with a mermaid floating above it, holding up the weight of the world on her shoulders, her second sight, pregnant with an idea, a waiting door. It was called *Transition* and seemed to represent birth amidst turmoil. *This one can stay.*

Next to *Transition* hung a small box frame containing my long-lost childhood marbles, which had been unearthed along with the little Wendy drawings now hanging in the bathroom. I peered at the still-sparkling clearies, cloudy tiger-eyes, and opaque black-and-whites. I could smell second-grade pavement, feel the anticipation of connection as I took my best shot, hear the clicking, feel the euphoria of winning. I had been good at playing marbles, until I wasn't. I'll be sure to hold on to these, I thought, smiling.

I sat down at my desk. I stared out the window, overlooking peaceful Sausalito Bay. It had been a long time since I had considered what it was that I really wanted. I knew what I didn't want, and taking my lonely, wistful paintings off the walls might be a start, but where did I go from here? What to do with my blank walls? What did I want my future to look like? Feel like? What was my story to be?

I sat in blank reflection, staring out over the water, letting my mind off its leash, like a dog at the beach. After a bit, a tickle of an idea started to rise, like carbonation, and I felt a glimmer of excitement. I didn't know how to use a brush and canvas, but I was learning to paint verbal pictures, and suddenly, feeling as though it couldn't possibly wait one more minute, I put my feather duster aside, pulled up to my computer, and began to write.

V DAY

i **woke up** early this morning and stumbled out to the café across the street from my house for my once-a-day caffeine fix. "A single cappuccino to go, please," I said to my regular coffee guy, Gerard. As I was ordering it, my single cappuccino, I suddenly felt immensely and nakedly *single,* as in "all alone." I order the same thing every morning, and I've never had this particular sensation before. It was like I was mocking myself. I wonder why? I'm no more or less single today than I was yesterday, so why was the word *single* suddenly significant? When a word or a phrase catches my eye (or my ear), sometimes I'll play word games with myself to see where my thinking is headed (or what my head is thinking). If it's headed in the wrong direction, I sometimes try to cut if off at the pass (my thinking, not my head). I considered the connotations of *single* while I waited for my coffee: Single-minded. Single-handed. Single-spaced. Single-breasted. A journey of a thousand miles starts with a single step. One for the road. Party of one. Back to square one. One bad apple spoils the bunch. One is the loneliest number. One wrong move, and you're dead. One flew over the cuckoo's nest.

Yikes! Not much liking where this train of thought was going, I considered what ordering a double might mean: Double the pleasure, double the fun. Double-breasted. Double down. Doubled over. Double jeopardy. Double-crossed. Double-dealing. Double agent. Double bed. Double trouble. Double vision. Dos Equis. Hmm, interesting. One road leads to the loony bin and the other leads to a drink. Not good. I wasn't fully awake yet and could only think in one-liners. God, it's too early for this, I thought, picking up my cappuccino and stirring sugar into the foamy heart design topping my drink, artfully provided by Gerard.

"Thanks for the heart," I said as I paid for my cappuccino (in singles) and tipped him.

"You are welcome, Wendy," he replied, adding, "Happy Valentine's Day!"

Ah, of course, now I remember. It's Valentine's Day.

I left the café and walked along the pier of Sausalito Bay until I found a bench where I could sit and look out at Dan Francisco, I mean San Francisco Day, I mean Bay. Dan Francisco Day—nice, Wendy, I thought, setting my coffee down next to me on the bench and rubbing my face with my hands.

Dan. When am I going to stop thinking about this guy? Why does V Day now have to mean He Day? We only dated for four months, but they had been intense, like a lifetime, and he was still embedded in me, I in him.

Okay, let's see, I thought. We broke up three weeks ago, so that means, based on my PMS (post-man syndrome) experience, if I considered the intensity of our experience, along with my willingness to utilize my life-support crew, my "Team Wendy" (including friends, workout buddies, my therapist, acupuncturist, massage therapist, yoga teacher, AA sponsor, and several twelve-step meetings a week—I am, after all, a Marin County resident), and factor in when my period is supposed to start, I'd say best case it will be, what, another few centuries before I feel much better? Ugh. How can I speed up this process? I absently glanced at my cell phone to see if I had any messages. The worst thing about carrying a cell phone is that no matter where you are, you know he hasn't called. But the one good thing about being single on Valentine's Day is that nobody can break up with me on Valentine's Day, I thought, and sipped my coffee. And I don't have to wear a thong.

While I sat in mourning reflection, a virgin sunrise was disrobing right before my eyes. I pulled out my tiny digital camera and took a few shots of the sleepy sweet new sky. I usually carry this camera around. I'm often searching for a perspective other than my own, and I can sometimes find one through a lens. A picture, after all, is worth a thousand words. I also take a lot of pictures of myself, holding the camera at arm's length (where my boyfriends can also usually be found). I snapped a few self-portraits now, with the sunrise as my backdrop. My friends have always given me a hard time about this habit, teasing me about being vain, but it's not vanity. I started doing it years ago, before digital cameras were even around, because I wanted some kind of indisputable evidence that I was actually there. I was always surprised when someone acknowledged me because most of the time I felt like I was invisible. Twenty years ago, I used a Polaroid and was always impatient for the picture to come into focus. I love the instant gratification of the digital era.

Yep, still here, I thought, absently looking at the woman in the photo. The sky in the background looked beautiful, almost more so in the camera than it did unveiling right in front of me. That's weird, I thought as I put the camera back in my pocket. That kind of thinking reminds me of looking at pictures of myself taken twenty, even thirty, years ago. I look at those photos now and I see a beautiful young woman, and I think, Look how lovely she is. I wish she'd known! But very often my perspective is so distorted that I can't appreciate what I actually have when I have it because I'm too focused on what I don't have. Especially back then, when I was still an active alcoholic and bulimic. I've noticed that the pictures that I've taken of myself have gotten better over the years, or maybe I've learned to love the lens, or the photographer has grown to love the subject, I'm not sure. Maybe I've just become kinder while viewing them. My challenge now seems to be learning to apply that principle to the three-dimensional Wendy, the real-time woman instead of the model/actress who portrays Wendy in her very own reality series on the Lifetime network. I often got these two confused, like the Doublemint twins. Who was who?

Attempting to acknowledge real-time Wendy, I said, *Who's the prettiest girl?* to myself, while pinching my cheeks, like a deranged Auntie Mame, and smiling. I closed my eyes and felt the pinch on my cheeks and the warmth of the sun, and for a few minutes I was happy. Like I was on a commercial break.

After a while, a young couple strolled by, pushing a baby carriage with a big pink heart-shaped Valentine balloon tied to it that said "Be Mine." As I watched them walk by, I felt a twinge of something I'd started feeling lately whenever I saw what I perceived to be a happy couple, and it didn't make me feel like the prettiest girl. Envy.

More like "Bee Mine," I said to myself as the sting of my unhappy ending with Dan returned. In the end, Dan had chosen to *be* with another woman. This had been inconceivable to me. In my mind, that meant that he had chosen her over me, and after a short while it was just too painful to continue. He and I had such a powerful connection and such explosive chemistry that I couldn't imagine why he would want to be with someone else. I wanted to be the one and only. My abandonment and betrayal issues had flared up, and now my heart was cramped and infected with grief. I felt I had been careless with my heart. It had been pried open, and now, instead of soaring, it was just sore.

My friend Hedy pointed out, "He didn't choose her over you—you chose him over you." In theory, I knew this to be true. That occasionally, once in a blue moon (*right!*), I lose my way in relationships with inappropriate men. I attract them and then dance my way over all the red flags on the battlefield, and with my white flag waving and my ass shaking, I surrender to the losing side. And then I get all Stockholm syndrome–ish and become attached to my captures, regardless of the danger that *I* have placed myself in. I *knew* all this intellectually, but right now all I could *feel* was the intense pain of withdrawal. I couldn't help it. I missed him.

And the fact that I'm feeling so sorry for myself, I thought, while sitting here basking in the astonishing beauty of this San Francisco Bay morning, well, that's the *single* most upsetting thing of all. Normally when I'm *sans* man on Valentine's Day, I save morbid reflection and self-pity for later in the evening, like a sickeningly rich dessert after a good meal, but I guess I was getting an early start this year. Dessert in the morning. Breakfast of champions. Stop freaking yourself out and think about something else before you make yourself really sick, I thought as I stood up, tossed my empty cappuccino cup into the garbage, and started back to get ready for my day.

When I got home, the first thing I did was get on my knees and pray. I hadn't done this for a while, gotten on my knees (while praying anyway), but harboring vindictive and obsessive thoughts about Dan was wearing me out and making me crazier than I usually am, so I called on my God Squad for help.

God, thank you in advance for relieving me of all obsessive thinking about Dan. I wish him the best and harbor no ill will toward him. (I find praying in gratitude, as though something were already so, helpful. I can't easily define what I'm praying to, but the act of prayer and the humility involved in getting on my knees provide relief, like opening a window in a stuffy room. I had nothing to lose other than my pain, and I felt almost ready to part with that.) Hmm, I thought, for the first time since we broke up, this actually *feels* true, like I really do wish him the best. Good. Better. I continued, *And bless that skanky little trailer trash ho that he's probably fucking as we speak.* Okay, clearly not completely healed, but moving in the right direction.

I got up, got dressed, and rifled through my collection of greeting cards, looking for appropriate Valentine's cards for my gal-pal lunch dates, Cameron and Jane, when I came across several somewhat hostile non-Hallmark cards that I must have purchased post-breakup. Probably not appropriate for a Hallmark holiday, I thought, flipping through them. One card showed a stereotypical woman from the fifties staring dreamily into space, with a caption reading, "She liked imaginary men best of all." Another from this series, which showed a woman leaning seductively against a tree and smoking, had the caption: "She had not yet decided whether to use her power for good . . . or for evil." Another showed a woman getting into a taxicab and telling the driver, "Take me to my next relationship, and step on it!" Another thoughtfully proclaimed, "She could no longer pretend that he wasn't an idiot." And finally, my personal favorite, one with a picture of a shoe, which said, "Fuck love, all you really need is a great pair of shoes." Then I noticed that there wasn't even a pair of shoes on the card, just one shoe, and it was a ruby-red slipper at that. Didn't Dorothy need both her shoes to click together in order to get home? It seemed I was always trying to find my way "home" by running away from home. That's funny, I thought, but none of these cards seemed right, even for my twisted friends. I didn't want to infect anyone else with my current bad attitude, like a jilted squid spewing gloomy boyfriend ink all over everybody's festive Valentine's Day, but somehow just reading the cards made me feel just the tiniest bit better, in a sick, Leona Helmsley sort of way. I left the one with the single shoe on my desk and threw the rest back into a drawer. Maybe I'll find someone who can appreciate the irony of that one, I thought as I grabbed my purse and a couple of sweet cards for my friends and headed out the door.

My first stop was therapy with Rita.

"Why is this so painful?" I asked as I rehashed my feelings about leaving Dan. This one seemed particularly difficult, as it was all tangled up with the anniversary of my mother's suicide. Normally separating from someone was hard for me, but my internal reaction this time seemed beyond reason, and the two events had become intertwined. I was still that betrayed child, torn away from her mother. But I was a woman as well, and needed to reconcile the two.

"It's a post-traumatic-syndrome reaction," she said. "An

overreaction to an event in the present that has triggered an emotional reaction to a traumatic event from the past." I knew this, but somehow that didn't make it any easier.

"Am I ever going to get better?" I asked, tearing up for a moment and feeling rather hopeless. "Must I be forever single in order to avoid this separation anxiety and trauma?" I said. "Will I ever be in a relationship that doesn't have to end?"

"You *are* getting better, right now. You are healing by feeling," she said.

I hate this part, I thought, the feeling part. And why did it always have to involve feeling *bad* instead of *good*?

"I'm just going to have to take your word for that right now," I said, sniffing.

Maybe the pain of walking through the fire is different from the pain of staying in the fire, but right now I couldn't tell the difference. It all felt like pain. I guess the difference was where you ended up. It feels like I'm bringing forth a new life, I thought; I just hope I don't die in childbirth.

I left therapy, and driving into the city for lunch, passed a woman hitchhiker with a cardboard sign that said "North." Doesn't she know she's on the wrong side of the highway? Traffic on this side is heading south. She'll never get where she's going if she stays there, I thought.

While waiting at a stoplight on Dan Ness, I mean Van Ness, Street in San Francisco on my way to the restaurant (damn, when is this V Day going to stop being a He Day!?), I glanced down and fingered the blue and brown silk dress I was wearing. Blue and brown, I thought, kind of like a healing bruise. Just like me. Then I remembered that this dress was from a clothing line called Single. How oddly perfect. And weird. Was this to be a day full of signs? Was I being singled out? And if so, wasn't it up to me to choose the interpretation? Being singled out could mean being a chosen one or being discriminated against. Which was it to be, Wendy?

Suddenly I felt something shift inside, and I paused, then took out my camera and looked at my digital reflection from this morning. A dim forty-watt bulb came on in my head, and I had a thought: What if I have been using the pain that I create with these relationships to prove to myself that I'm real, in the same way that I take pictures of myself to prove that I'm still here? Is this what Rita was saying, that I must feel to heal to be real? Am I real enough yet?

The stoplight turned green, and I had started moving the car forward, when my phone rang. Questions were still swirling around my dimly lit head, and I was busy squinting for answers, so I didn't look at the caller ID as I picked up the call.

"Hello," I said.

"Hi," he said. "Happy Valentine's Day."

Ouch, I thought, feeling like he had just poked my bruise. Yep, I'm real, all right.

"Gee, thanks, Dan," I replied, and catching my tone, he paused, not sure how to proceed. But then I took a deep breath and exhaled, softening up a little. We hadn't spoken for weeks, and in the interim I had mailed him an angry letter. You know, the kind of venting letter that you write but should never send? I wrote it early on a Saturday morning when I was really upset and angry after having nightmares of him with the other woman (psychic enmeshment is a bitch) and mailed it on my way to an Al-Anon meeting. I knew if I waited until after the meeting I wouldn't have sent it. I knew better, but did it anyway. The sentiments in the letter may have been true, and he may have "deserved" it, but ultimately, mailing it was like chewing Juicy Fruit gum. It was only sweet for a minute before leaving a bad artificial taste that still lingered in my mouth. This was an opportunity to get rid of that nasty aftertaste, regardless of what his behavior had been, so I apologized for sending the letter (although not for the contents!). He told me that he was sorry that he hurt me and that he missed me. My intuition told me that he was fishing to see whether or not I was still willing to have sex with him, in spite of everything that had happened, and although part of me still honest-to-God wanted to, another growing part, the groggily illuminated part, knew better. So instead of engaging him in a lengthy discussion, I thanked him for calling and got off the phone. It felt good to be the one to end the call, for real.

Maybe I wasn't really heading south after all.

I met Cameron and Jane at Le Charme on Fifth Street, and we exchanged little gifts and cards. I still felt anxious and a little shaky from my Dan call, but something like awareness was flickering in me now, like a loose naked bulb in a dark hallway.

As I looked over the menu, I noticed the word: *men*u. I just can't seem to separate men and you, I thought to myself, but this time I laughed.

"Wouldn't it be great if there were special positive-affirmation menus for V Day [or He Day] sufferers," I said, "like a special "Shift Happens" menu with stuff like Perspective Petrale, Humility Hummus, or Forgiveness French Fries?"

My friends looked at me blankly. This was a little too twelve-steppy for them, and Jane countered, "What about a Heartbroken Hamburger or Fuck You French Fries?"

Wow, I thought, maybe I should have given Jane that card after all!

But we all laughed.

"I'll have the bitter greens," I told our waiter, "and a blood sausage Danwich, I mean, sandwich."

"Better bring her some lemonade, too," Cameron said.

"Make it a double," I said, laughing again.

Cameron went on to describe some difficulties in her relationship and how she was attending *un*couples counseling later that day to get some help sorting it out. (BTW, does everyone these days have therapy on Valentine's Day?) Jane recounted stories from her recent book tour in New York and how it felt to be riding a wave of success while grieving in other areas of her life. We laughed a little and cried a little as I shared my bitter greens and they shared theirs.

I sat watching them talk, sipping my double lemonade,

when a new feeling for the day emerged, and as I felt this immense *love* for my friends take hold, the single naked bulb in
my hallway began to hold steady and burn brighter.

He Day had just turned into We Day.

when i got home from lunch, I ate a few heart-
shaped Dove chocolate candies made especially for Valentine's
Day. Each one had a little message on the inside, and I ate
several of them, looking for the next "sign." I ate my way
through "Trust with your heart, not your head" and
"Chocolate always loves you back," before I got two in a row
of "Be your own Valentine." Hmm. Be my own Valentine. Be
'tine. Be mine. Like the heart-shaped balloon from this morning. What a concept. Okay, I thought, let's put sarcastic Wendy
aside for a minute and go with this one. What if I were to be
mine, and mine alone? What do I think I need to hear from a
man or from another in order to feel loved? What do I need to
hear from myself? What would happen if I tried to officially
give me to myself? Would I throw me back in my face and slam
the door? Would I vote myself off of my own island? Had I ever
even tried?

Go for it, I said, *you have my permission,* and before my
mind could mobilize a defense against me, I wrote down everything that I wanted to hear at that moment in what appeared
to be my format for the day: one-liners.

I am sorry.

I was wrong.

You were right.

I didn't realize what I had until you were gone.

I missed you. I missed us.

I will never leave you again.

I am here for you, always.

You matter more to me than anything else in the world.

I can't live without you.

I want you.

I need you.

You are my sweetheart.

You are wonderful.

I'm darn-right crazy about you.

You are so beautiful.

I'm so lucky to have you in my life.

I can't believe you chose me.

There is nobody else like you.

You make me a better person.

You are perfect just as you are.

The world is a better place when you are near.

*I want to wake up next to you every morning and go to
    sleep in your arms every night.*

I will be there for you no matter what.

I trust you. I admire you. I respect you. I desire you.

You are amazing.

You are the love of my life.

You are my happily ever after.
You are the only one for me.
You complete me.
I love you.
You are the one.

I read the list several times, slowly, but I was barely breathing. About the sixth time through, I actually stopped feeling silly, remembered to breathe, and started to *feel* both loving and loved. It wasn't prose, but it was hitting the spot. I knew it was hokey, but I didn't care. I read it through one more time, out loud. I had spent too much time trying to inspire others to say these things to me and mean them, and it felt amazing to hear them, even from me—scratch that, especially from me. Even more amazing was that I was able to allow these words in, overwriting other words that had been permanent occupants of this space. These residents were ideas like *You can't be trusted, Everyone you love will leave you, You aren't lovable, You aren't worthy, YOU WILL NEVER BE GOOD ENOUGH.* I had tried everything to make these tenants happy. I'd repainted, bought new furniture, fed them, clothed them, got them drunk, and entertained their sleazy friends, but still they lived in squalor and wouldn't pay the rent. Maybe it was high time to evict these squatters, clean house, and make amends to the landlord.

We Day was becoming Me Day.

Inspired by these one-liners, I sat down to write a special

Valentine poem to *the one* who I hoped would still be in my life next year at this time. The poem was hokey, but I knew she would like it. When I finished, I printed out the picture of myself from this morning's sunrise and slipped the picture and the poem into the "Fuck Love" card that I had left out for that special someone before sealing it with a kiss. I knew the recipient would appreciate the irony. I wrote, "Not to be opened until Valentine's Day 2008." I hope this is well-received, I thought, and put it in my purse to mail.

my next valentine pit stop was a Quirky Alone party in San Francisco that was being held at an old-man bar called Jack's in a warehouse neighborhood. Quirky Alone was a movement of sorts for idiosyncratic types who liked their aloneness and therefore ostensibly themselves. I wasn't sure I was on board with the whole concept. I liked my aloneness just fine but didn't really want to brand myself that way. Still, I was curious, and when I went to the website and took the Quirky Alone test, I did score 100, so apparently I was more than qualified. (I later learned, to my immense relief, that 100 didn't mean 100 percent, but 100 points out of many more.)

When I got there, it was as advertised, a funky old-man's bar that had been primarily taken over for the evening by what appeared to be a nice-looking crowd of yuppies. I got a name tag and wandered around for a bit, but it felt like yet another singles mixer where everybody was checking one another out. How ironic. I usually feel like a giant doofus at these types of events, but tonight I was still basking in the reflective warmth of my afternoon. I headed to the bar to order a soda water, when I noticed three men who looked like regulars stationed at the end of the bar, the kind of drunks who belonged in an old-man bar early on a Wednesday night. They looked kind of stunned, as though their planet had just been invaded by aliens, and were attempting to keep a low profile, lest they be discovered. These were my kind of people, I thought as I walked over to their side of the planet and slapped my hand on the bar, saying, "Hello, gentlemen, how are you three doing tonight?" I was feeling feisty now!

Startled out of their stupors and happy to be noticed, they perked up and said their hellos.

"You three look like the Holey [with an *e*] Trinity," I said. "Which one of you is which?"

They laughed, and we assigned identities: the Father, the Son, and the Holey Ghost.

They were each in various stages of drunkenness, but they were friendly drunks, so they bought me a soda water and asked me about myself. I told them I was writing a book.

"What's the name of the book?" asked the Holey Ghost.

"Falling into Manholes," I said.

He looked at me like he'd seen a ghost.

"How did you know that I worked in manholes?" he asked in all sincerity, as only a drunk who doesn't think much of himself but is all he thinks about can.

"You worked in manholes?" I replied, and smiled. "Please, tell me all about them."

He went on to tell us how dark and dirty and stinky manholes were, with lots of sewage and rats and other vermin, and how when poisonous gas collected in them they would sometimes blow their lids, and how you couldn't be too careful while in the manhole, and how you could even get killed down there.

"A manhole for me is a nasty place to be," he finished, and took a swig of his beer.

"I know what you mean," I said, and he looked like he believed me.

The Father and the Son ordered another round, and the Holey Ghost glanced at my soda water.

"Why aren't you drinking?" he asked.

"I've been sober in AA for almost eighteen years now," I said.

"Really?" he said, and his eyes got big before he turned back to his beer.

"Yup," I replied. "April first is my sobriety birthday. I'm almost legal!" And we both laughed.

I didn't often answer this question with my sobriety qualifications, but for some reason, tonight I had. I guess it was the right thing to say because the Holey Ghost started telling me how he had been fired by the utility company because of his drinking. He told me how at one point he'd been sober in AA for about a year, and even though he didn't think the program worked, he remembered that year as a happy one. But then he started drinking again, and even though manholes were nasty, he wished he could get his job back.

"Go ahead," he said, "lay it on me," and sort of hunched down over his beer like I was going to give him a proper AA tongue-lashing.

"It's funny, isn't it," I said, "that you are looking to get back into manholes and I'm trying to stay out of them." I added, "I'm just glad that neither one of us got killed while we were down there."

He looked sideways at me and smiled.

"Listen," I said softly, "if drinking still worked for me, I would still be doing it. For today, I'm just trying to stay above ground where the light is. You know what I mean?" I asked, and he nodded and swallowed his beer.

I looked around the bar and realized that there was nothing else for me here tonight. I had met the *me*n I was meant to meet, and now it was time to take flight.

"It was such a pleasure meeting you all," I said, shaking hands before my exit.

"It's been real," the Holey Ghost said as he waved good-bye, and I knew he really meant it.

my final stop that evening was an AA meeting where I was scheduled to speak on the twelfth step. (Having had a spiritual awakening as a result of these steps, we tried to carry this message to other alcoholics and practice these principles in all our affairs.) I had been looking forward to this all day. No matter what's going on in my life, when I'm able to show up and be of service, *somehow* I get a reprieve from my thinking long enough for something else to get in there, and, well, when I'm really lucky, shift happens.

It was a small meeting in San Rafael, and as I settled into my seat, I began to relax. I never notice how truly wound up I get during my day until I'm in a meeting. Tonight it was like slipping into a warm bath at the end of a long day and feeling the release of tension that I didn't even know I had, as overworked muscles that try to hold it all together start letting go, one by one.

When it was time for the speaker portion of the meeting, I stood up in the front of the room to share in a general way what I was like when I drank, what happened, and what I'm like now. For some reason, this time I talked more than usual about when I was young. My duplicity and sugar addiction as a child, my mom's death when I was sixteen, my eating disorders as a teenager, and my love affair with alcohol in my early twenties. Then I shared how one day, alcohol just turned on me, like a jealous lover, and how I couldn't believe it, and it was a big fat bummer. I described what it felt like at that intersection of desperation and despair and how I did the most radical thing I have ever done: I asked for help. I talked about my alcoholic thinking, and how I try to solve my problems with the same thinking that creates the problems and how that doesn't work. How I came to believe that the solution to my problems is beyond my imagination and how I try to stay open to what I don't understand. How it never seems to be about what I need to get but what I need to let go of. How hard it is for me to let go, and how I leave claw marks in everything. How I've learned to constantly redirect my thinking and how I've come to think of a miracle as a shift in perception. How when I team up with this power greater than myself that I don't understand and can't control, something wonderful happens and transformation occurs. How in order to stay sober I'm learning to take responsibility for my thoughts and my actions instead of blaming everybody else, and how much better that feels. How learning to say and hear the truth, no matter how painful, opens me up to infinite possibility. How I'm always learning about what honesty means and how to keep my house clean instead of spending as much time trying to clean other people's houses. How forgiveness doesn't make the other person right, it just makes me free. How to practice stuff that feels weird at first, like praying to this higher power and learning to call it God without freaking myself out because it's easier than saying "a power greater than myself" all the time, and learning how to tune in and listen to God talk radio. How this program has taught me how to live one day at a time without alcohol or drugs and how I continue to learn how to apply principles like willingness and acceptance and humility and surrender and forgiveness to my life so that I don't have to drink and I don't have to be afraid *all* of the time. How the shorthand for recovery is being of service in any way I can, in and out of the rooms of AA, and how fun it is finding out what that means. How important it is to know that I don't have to do something just because I feel like it (drink), and I don't have to wait until I feel like it to do something (go to a meeting). How I'm an endless work-in-progress, like the Big Dig in Boston. How as a result of all of this I have been relieved of the desire to drink, or starve myself, or eat and throw up, or take drugs, and how that's a *miracle*. How sometimes I am so joyous that I feel like if I died on the spot it would be okay.

In a nutshell, I shared how I live sober and how the program of AA has radically changed my life and how the fellowship of AA loved me until I began to love myself, and how the newcomer is the single most important person in the room.

I ended by quoting one of my favorite lines by Robert Frost: "We dance round in a ring and suppose, / But the Secret sits in the middle and knows." I jammed all of this into my allotted time because I talk fast and I'm wound tight, and my head was on fire with words that day, and by the time I sat down I wasn't anxious anymore, and even though I had been talking about myself for fifteen minutes, I wasn't thinking about myself, and I was happy.

After my share, the meeting was open for sharing from the room. In this meeting, people raise their hands, and I called on them. A few men shared, but I kept glancing in the corner, where a young woman, maybe twenty years old, sat, all shiny and new. She had announced at the beginning of the meeting that she had ninety days sober today, and we had all clapped.

"Do any females in the room want to share?" I asked, trying not to look directly at her.

A few minutes later, she tentatively raised her hand, and I called on her.

"Hi, my name is Lily, and I'm an alcoholic."

"Hi, Lily," everyone said.

"I never talk that much in meetings," she said nervously, "but ever since I came to AA, people have been telling me that I will hear my story in the rooms, but I never have. *Until now.* Tonight you told my story. I really related to everything you said and how you felt when you were little and your mom's death and the eating disorders and how you tried to act tough but how scared and lonely you were and how you wanted to drink until you passed out so you wouldn't feel anything. I wanted to thank you so, *so* much; you are an inspiration to me. Thank you."

Her voice shook, but her eyes shone, and as she finished I could see that she had at that moment the one thing that she needed most of all: hope.

As I was listening to her speak, I felt tears being drawn from a wellspring, heading for the surface, and I caught my breath.

Where before my head had been on fire, my heart was now ablaze, and the naked flickering bulb in my hallway was replaced with a room full of light. As much light as I could possibly hold, I could have. I was a clean, well-lighted place. I was a room with a view. I was Batteries, Bulbs, and Beyond. I was hooked up to the mother lode of all generators. I was connected to that current that is always there, like radio waves, but I can't always find the station, or I get a staticky signal, or I completely forget to tune in. There was no anxiety, no loneliness, no thoughts of Dan or what I did or did not have. I didn't want for anything, and it was no longer about me. Me Day was transforming into Thee Day, and all my grief and fear and bullshit was morphing into something that felt like love, real love. I was there in that moment with that young woman in the corner, Lily, who had ninety days sober and was reaching toward the light, and the light was in me and all around me, and I loved her, I loved everyone in that room, and I was filled with grace and so, so grateful to be a sober alcoholic. Shift happened, and a bigger, brighter space than I ever thought possible for me was suddenly available for occupancy, and as the double-wide doors of my chest opened up to greet it, my one and only heart flew free, to meet it.

BREAKFAST EPIPHANIES

1ast night my friend Cameron and I went to an event at Foreign Cinema, a trendy French bistro tucked away in a dingy neighborhood of San Francisco, where they project old movies onto a brick wall in a covered patio area for diners to enjoy *sans* sound. Our event was in a separate room, but as we were leaving, we stopped in the patio and stood under a heat lamp in the chilly evening to watch the end of the movie that was playing, the classic *Breakfast at Tiffany's* with Audrey Hepburn as Holly Golightly and George Peppard as Paul "Fred" Varjak. I had seen the movie years ago and remembered the story line well.

Holly was a pretty, quirky young woman on the run from herself and her unhappy childhood in Podunk, Texas. She had fled to New York City, where she constructed a sophisticated, sexy, socialite persona, taking many lovers and living the "high" life (she was basically an ingénue hooker). Her roommate was a stray cat she simply called Cat, because she couldn't commit to the idea that he was hers by giving him a real name. As the movie unfolds, the viewer comes to see that Holly couldn't own anything or belong to anyone because she had disowned herself and focused instead on being desired by men. Whenever Holly got really frightened and didn't know why, she would take a cab to Tiffany's, the only place where she felt truly safe.

In the movie, a young writer, Paul, whom she always calls Fred, moves in next door and gets swept into Holly's world of parties and socializing but also comes to know the fragile, vulnerable girl that lives beneath her glossy veneer. They fall in love, but Holly is determined to keep him at arm's length, heralding herself as a wild, free thing that can't be tamed or fenced in.

Cameron and I walked in during the last scene, when Holly is in a taxi with Cat and Fred. Holly is trying to run away again, and Fred is trying to stop her. To prove to Fred that she doesn't need anybody or anything, she throws Cat out of the cab into the pouring rain and slams the door. At this, Fred loses it and jumps out of the cab, and we read his lips as he says, "You know what's wrong with you, Miss Whoever-you-are? You're chicken. You've got no guts. You're afraid to stick out your chin and say, 'Okay, life's a fact, people do fall in love, people do belong to each other, because that's the only chance anybody's got for real happiness.' You call yourself a free spirit, a 'wild thing,' and you're terrified somebody's gonna stick you in a cage. Well, baby, you're already in that cage. You built it yourself. It's wherever you go. Because no matter where you run, you just end up running into yourself."

Then he throws a simple engagement ring into her lap, the one that he bought her at Tiffany's and had been carrying around for months, and goes off to find Cat.

Holly sits in the cab shaking, at odds with herself, as always, and we witness her epiphany. Her false persona breaks down, and she sees what she has done, realizes that by throwing Cat into the rainy night, she is throwing herself away, that she has been pushing away anyone or anything that really matters. By being afraid to lose love, she has lost a chance for love and, even more important, her self. She puts the ring on with shaking hands and flings herself out of the cab in the pouring rain, then runs down the street. She catches up to Fred and says, "Where's Cat?" He doesn't know, and she stumbles into an alley, screaming, "Cat, Cat!" like her life depends on it, rummaging through empty boxes in the rain, scrounging through garbage in a forgotten alley, looking for the one thing that matters. "Cat, Cat, CAT!"

Cameron and I stand there, gripping each other, imploring, "Cat, Cat, CAT!" right along with her, providing the soundtrack for the nearby diners. As Holly stands there in the pouring rain, in this desolate alley, she starts to despair, and we start to despair with her, when, suddenly, Cat pops his wet little head out of a box right in front of her and meows tentatively, and we all catch our breath as Holly scoops him up and holds him dear to her heart, sobbing now, as though she has just found her beloved.

Cameron and I stand among the diners in this outdoor venue and struggle not to cry, not to make a spectacle of ourselves, and fail. "I love this movie," we say simultaneously, and hug each other there in the open air under the heat lamps with Holly Golightly and Cat and Fred and of course all of the patio diners who were treated to our live performance at Foreign Cinema that night.

Then we watched as Holly stumbles back to Fred, who has been waiting at the entry to the alley, and they kiss with Cat pressed between them in the rain. That may have been the "Hollywood" ending, but the real happily-ever-after moment for me is Holly *wanting* Cat and Holly *finding* Cat and Holly *loving* Cat, knowing that Cat is Holly and Holly is Cat.

True, I may have been premenstrual, but it is no mystery why this movie resonates with me. I've come to see how I've spent a good part of my life throwing my "Cat" out into the rain, and have only recently come to find her, only now begun to know how to love her. As I have been writing this memoir, writing about my life, I have gone back and looked for the little girl, the teenager, and the young woman that I was, and have reclaimed myself all along the way, like a human SPCA.

After Cameron and I said good night, I wandered around for a while looking for my car. I felt disoriented and couldn't for the life of me remember where I was parked. As I walked up and down the deserted street in this scary neighborhood on this wintry San Francisco night looking for my ride home, I repeated, "Cat, Cat, Cat," softly to myself until I finally found my car, which had, incidentally, been in very close proximity all along. It felt good to come in out of the cold and know that within minutes I would be warm again and safely on my way home.

Tucked in my bed that night, I dreamed that I wandered into a deserted alley I had never seen, even though it was adjacent to a street that I had walked down many, many times before. At the end of the alley, there was a man waiting to greet me and usher me into some kind of magical movie theater. He was welcoming and friendly and handed me a ticket to enter the theater and see the show.

"It's not often that someone stumbles across this place unless they are looking for it," he said as he led me toward the door. I intuitively liked and trusted him. He seemed loving and kind, and he glowed, like a modern-day ticket-dispensing version of Jesus.

As he opened the door for me, he smiled, and I entered the darkened room. Inside was a huge, bright Technicolor IMAX display, and as my eyes adjusted to the dark, I began to pay attention to what was being revealed before me. As I stood there, surrounded by the gentle flickering light, it slowly dawned on me that I wasn't watching a movie at all, it was more like watching real life, *my* real life, and I woke up feeling peaceful, as though I finally understood that, having already been given the ticket, all I really needed to do now was go to the show.

acknowledgments

I seem to be having trouble writing this without it sounding like one of those dreadful Academy Award acceptance speeches delivered by some unknown writer who has obviously spent *way* too much time alone, so if you aren't skimming this section for your name, you might just want to skip it!

Having said that (I say, pulling a wad of paper from my Wonderbra with trembling hands), I'd like to thank Karen Bouris for taking a chance on me and subsequently publishing my very first essay; my current editor, Neil Nyren, for listening to my pitch for this book with a straight face and giving me a shot; my agent, Robert Stricker, for believing in me, and pointing me in the right direction; and the island of Maui for somehow facilitating it all.

I could not have written this without the support of Betsy,

Habeeba, Kristen, Marco, Janet, Holly, and Borys, who kept my marketing business afloat while I explored and documented my insanity (of which I am sure they are all too aware).

For my friends, Kathy, Hedy, Maria, Kristen, Diane, Vanya, Leslie, Dana, Racine, Sandra, Jerry, Medora, Kim, Michele, Larissa, Jenny, Gina, Cynthia, Gwendolyn, Emily, Dorka, Alan, Parker, and Barb, who all, at one time or another, said something clever that I have probably since co-opted, tolerated my obsessive nature, and encouraged me always to just "write that down!" For everyone and anyone in "the rooms," whose faces alone have sometimes kept me sober. For my funny and brilliant sisters, Vicki, Robin, and Christina, for their timeless love and support, and my father, for loving me even after reading this book. For all the men in my life, past and present, without whom this would have been a decidedly different book.

And since writing this book has felt like giving birth (to myself), I especially want to thank Jane, April, and Kathi for encouraging me through the morning sickness; Cameron and Kristen for helping to deliver the baby; Kaye and Rita for keeping me from dying during childbirth; and to VISA, for providing retail therapy during the postpartum depression.

Let me finish by saying (as the music is blaring me off the stage) that I do not speak for AA or any other twelve-step program; I've simply tried to share my experience. The events in this book are true, or as true as my memory of them can possibly be, but names have been changed to protect the not-so-innocent, and time lines have sometimes been rearranged and characters occasionally combined or revised in the service of telling the story. Rest assured that the feelings expressed throughout are, unquestionably, all mine (after all, who else would possibly want them?).

WENDY MERRILL runs WAM Marketing Group, a marketing communications company based in Sausalito, California, where she lives aboveground and beyond her means. Two of her autobiographical essays have previously appeared in *Single Women of a Certain Age,* edited by Jane Ganahl, and *Single State of the Union,* edited by Diane Mapes. *Falling into Manholes* is Wendy's first book. Visit her website at www.fallingintomanholes.com.